SWEET CELEBRATIONS

SWEET
CELEBRATIONS
24 DESSERT PARTIES FOR EVERY OCCASION

PEGGY MELLODY

Photography by E. K. Waller

Taylor Publishing Company
Dallas, Texas

For Pat, Vicki, Judy, Sean, Joe, and Tim

Copyright © 1991 by Peggy Mellody

All rights reserved.

Published by Taylor Publishing Company
1550 West Mockingbird Lane
Dallas, Texas 75235

Designed by Whitehead & Whitehead

Photographer: E. K. Waller

Food Stylists: Alice M. Hart and Julie Madonia

Additional styling credits follow text.

Library of Congress Cataloging-in-Publication Data
Mellody, Peggy.
    Sweet celebrations : 24 dessert parties for every occasion / Peggy Mellody.
        p.   cm.
    Includes index.
    ISBN 0-87833-740-7 : $24.95
    1. Desserts. 2. Menus. 3. Entertaining. I. Title.
TX773.M45 1991
641.8′6—dc20   91-16366
                                                                        CIP

Printed in the United States of America
10   9   8   7   6   5   4   3   2   1

Acknowledgements

Without the following people this book would never have come together: my agents Elizabeth Pomada and Michael Larsen, who thought enough of the idea to make into a reality; my husband Barry Nackos, who put up with my erratic hours and mood swings; my father-in-law Gust Nackos, for his emergency computer service; Linda Zimmerman, who understood better than most what it was like to work under the pressure of having several projects due at the same time; Linda Rose, who always seemed to be in my corner; and my editors Mary Kelly and Holly McGuire for their constant optimism and words of support.

I would also like to give special thanks to Leslie Cohen, Nina Cohen, Alice M. Hart, Nancy Mellody, George Morrone, Cathy Thomas, Dana Wechter, Sue Young, and Linda Zimmerman for their recipes, taste buds, and inspiration.

Many people contributed their special gifts to this book. My staff E. K. Waller, Alice M. Hart, Julie Madonia, and Evelyn Hart were not only responsible for creating the beautiful photography in *Sweet Celebrations,* but they also took this project far beyond their contracted duties. My gratitude also goes to Sego Nursery, New Zealand Gourmet, California Strawberry Advisory Board, G & G Produce Company, Frieda's Finest, Peter Ritt of Washington-Oregon-California Pear Board, Bob Hecklau of L.A. Nut House, Art Options, Tesoro, Blueprint, Geary's, Mise en Place, Steve's, and Betty Ash of Compartes. I deeply appreciate the time, care, and energy they put into this book.

Finally, a special word of thanks to my parents for contributions far extending the work of this book.

Contents

Introduction

For most of us, dessert has a more profound meaning than this simple definition the dictionary gives it. We associate the word with twinkling eyes, moans and sighs, and visions of sweet gastronomic highs. Going without it can be brutal punishment to a child, sheer torture to a dieter. We are a nation obsessed with dessert—it's something we can't help loving.

Have you ever paced yourself through a meal in anticipation of the grand finale? Well, imagine not having to wait. Imagine a meal in which dessert would be the beginning. The middle. And the end. That's what dessert parties are all about.

A dessert buffet is the ultimate indulgence, a delicious alternative to the ubiquitous wine and cheese party or the traditional cocktail affair. With the decrease in alcohol consumption, dessert parties are becoming more and more attractive. To meet the growing demand for gourmet confections, many caterers, restaurants, and national hotels are featuring dessert buffets and high teas in place of conventional menus. As a host, why not play to this audience by setting a beautifully decorated table laden with spectacular desserts? *Sweet Celebrations* makes it easy.

Sweet Celebrations gives you nearly 150 recipes, ranging from traditional to contemporary desserts, which are straightforward yet sophisticated, appealing to novice and experienced cooks alike. Written with today's lifestyle in mind, many recipes can be made ahead and any of the 24 parties for 2 to 200 people can be planned in advance, ensuring you success without stress. Additionally, this complete guide provides you with an "All About Entertaining" section which answers commonly asked questions and offers valuable advice on handling ingredients and simplifying entertaining. The Party Countdown Calendar does the planning for you, so that even your very first dessert party comes off smoothly. Plus, the "Key Ingredients" chapter gives you some basic techniques for working with dessert ingredients so that all of your results have professional polish. Dessert menus need a balance of sweet and savory flavors, and cheeses provide a savory addition to any dessert party. The "Dessert Cheeses" chapter offers you a guide to matching cheeses with desserts for perfect results.

Divided into four seasonal sections—spring, summer, fall, and winter—*Sweet Celebrations* is a year-round cookbook. Each section gives you six complete parties for holidays and special occasions, as well as parties to have just for fun, such as the Nutcracker Tea and the Mid-Morning Muffin Break. Each menu provides the perfect combination of texture, flavor, and color, enhanced by the use of fresh, seasonal ingredients. There is a party here for every occasion, and you'll want to try them all. *Sweet Celebrations* guarantees that your parties will be stylish, impressive, and memorable.

SWEET CELEBRATIONS

1 All About Entertaining

Organization and careful planning are the keys to successful entertaining. When every detail is thought out and taken care of in advance, the host can feel like a guest when the big day or eve comes around, and that is the sign of a truly successful party. The moment you decide to throw a party is the time to begin planning. Here are the most important questions to consider:

1 How much should I spend?

Creating a budget is vital, and you should be realistic in doing so. Figure out exactly how much you can afford to spend and don't exceed that limit—it's hard to enjoy your party when all you can think of is how you'll pay for it. When planning your party budget, be sure to list all costs no matter how small they might be. Allow for flowers, decorations, food items, beverages, ice, equipment, invitations (including postage), anything else needed, plus an additional 10% of the entire budget for unforeseen expenses—they come up even for the most experienced of hosts.

2 Who and how many should I invite?

Deciding the names and number of people who make up your guest list is as important a factor as is your menu—both play a vital role in determining what the party will be like. When drawing up your guest list, consider the following points:
- The objective of the party. Are you having a party to reciprocate, to mix friends, or to gather business associates? Be careful about mixing friends and business associates. It doesn't always work.
- The age of your guests
- Your budget
- Your space/location. Will the party be at home, in a rental hall, or outdoors?

- The season. The time of year you host a party will affect the attendance. The peak holiday season is from Halloween to New Years. Generally, attendance for parties given during the off-season (January through May and September and October) is 80%, during the peak season 50%, and during the summer months 60%.
- The number of guests you will feel comfortable hosting

3 What about invitations?

Invitations should be issued one month in advance for large parties or for parties given during the holidays. For small, casual gatherings given in the off-season, two weeks notice is sufficient. In any case, either written or oral invitations are appropriate. If you send written invitations, be sure to request an R.S.V.P. to make your party planning easier. When an R.S.V.P. is not responded to within two weeks of the party, a phone call to the invitee is in order (gentle diplomacy is the key in this case). In whatever fashion you extend your invitations, be certain that all of them are issued on the same day. No one wants to feel that he was an afterthought. Last, but of utmost importance, make sure you include all specific information in your invitations: date, time, place, theme (when appropriate), attire (if special), map (if necessary), and special things to bring (i.e., a blanket to sit on for an outdoor party).

4 How do I plan a dessert menu?

The menu and the guest list are the two most important determiners of a successful party. Whether you use the dessert menus in this book or create your own, keep in mind the following guidelines:

- The purpose of the party: Is it for an anniversary, a promotion, or a shower?
- The theme of the party, such as Caribbean, Mardi Gras, or Bastille Day.
- The age of the guests. Older adults eat less than young adults and children.
- The sex of the guests. Men usually prefer simple but substantial desserts such as bar cookies, brownies, and cheesecake, while women often select pretty, elegant desserts.
- The time of day. This will affect the amount of food consumed. Parties held between meal times require less food. Guests will consume twice as much food at a party held at the dinner hour than a party held later in the evening.
- The season. Plan the menu to take full advantage of seasonal ingredients.
- The number of guests
- The capacity of your kitchen
- A blend of savory and sweet foods
- Your budget. Cost out all ingredients. The cost of desserts adds up quickly.
- The supplies needed
- Freezer and refrigerator space
- The location of the party

5 How do I calculate the number of servings from each menu?

The number of servings from each buffet is determined by the number of guests and the number of desserts. Keep in mind that all of your guests will want to taste several of the sweet offerings. As a result, a cheesecake when served alone may serve 12, but when served with other desserts can serve 18. The servings listed with each recipe in this book indicate how many people are served if the dessert is served alone.

An easy formula for figuring how many guests your buffet will accommodate is to total up the number of servings from each dessert and divide by three (i.e., 6 desserts × 10 servings each = 60, divided by 3 = 20 guests). Because guests will want more than one dessert, count on at least two to three 7- or 8-inch plates per person.

6 What are the best beverages to serve with desserts?

Choosing the proper beverage is an important decision for the host or hostess. Neither the food nor the drink should be overwhelming. Balance is the key. The perfect beverages to serve at a dessert party are ice water, coffee, and wine. To get you started on your beverage selection, here are some guidelines:
- *Water:* Have plenty of iced water (sparkling and nonsparkling) on hand, since sweets tend to make guests extra thirsty.
- *Coffee:* The fragrance of freshly brewed coffee is one of the most inviting in the world, and its mellow, full-bodied taste is among the most satisfying. Coffee and dessert are perfect together. The cup of coffee served is just as important as the food, so don't compromise on quality. Nothing ruins a good dessert like a bad cup of coffee. Serve freshly brewed caffeinated and decaffeinated coffee from top grade coffee beans.
- *Wine:* The subtle nuances of taste, sight, and smell in wine enhance any dessert. Wine is the ideal accompaniment to dessert. There are no strict rules governing wine/dessert matchups; let common sense and your preference be your guides. Although there

are many varieties of wine available, not all go well with desserts. Desserts call for wines that won't be overpowered by high levels of sugar. The solution is to use a crisp, sparkling wine such as champagne.

Fruit and light desserts pair well with sweet wines such as white Riesling, French sauterne, late harvest Riesling, muscat canelli, and German auslese. Desserts based on nuts or dried fruits are particularly nice with cream sherry, port, Madiera, and Marsala. Chocolate, the most difficult to match with wine, works with cabernet sauvignon, port, sherry, and brut champagne. When in doubt, serve champagne—it goes with any dessert.

Wine merchants can help you plan and choose the wines most appropriate for your party. Outline your budget, what you will be serving the wines with, and whether you are emphasizing the wine or the dessert.

The amount of wine to purchase varies depending upon the type of wine and how much your guests normally consume. In general, figure on ½ to 1 bottle of champagne per person, and 2 glasses of other dessert wines per person. Order wines at least two weeks in advance and arrange for wines to be delivered chilled the day of the party.

7 Do I need to hire help?

The purpose of hiring professional party help is to free the host to have fun and to socialize with guests. Agencies specializing in household personnel, caterers, and local restaurants are good resources for finding professional food servers. The size and type of party will determine the number of servers needed. In general, hire

1 server per buffet table or 3 waiters per 20 guests for seated service. Always hire a separate bartender or designate someone to be responsible for serving alcoholic beverages. For large parties, figure 1 bartender per 50 guests.

8   How should I arrange a dessert buffet?

The buffet is the easiest method of serving. A buffet table should be arranged so that the guests can serve themselves in the easiest way possible. Items should be arranged in a logical sequence in the buffet area. Start with napkins and plates on the buffet or on a side table near the beginning of the line, follow with a variety of desserts, and end with silverware and beverages. Place a printed menu at the beginning of the buffet table or a card next to each item naming the dessert. To encourage people to circulate, arrange several small buffets. Beverages are often better served in a separate area instead of at the end of the buffet.

Desserts should be served on serving dishes and trays that complement the shape and color of the particular sweet. Arrange desserts at different heights on the table. A catering trick used to create height is to take different sized cans (i.e., tomato soup cans, tuna fish cans, etc. . . .) and cover them with napkins. Only the host knows what is beneath the napkins. Serving trays are placed on top. Be sure when desserts are arranged on the table that there is enough room for guests to set down their dishes if they will be serving themselves.

9   What is the best way to serve desserts?

Always make sure there are enough serving utensils for each dessert. Cutting and serving some desserts can be very messy. Warm, dry knives make cutting and serving desserts easy. An easy way to warm knives is to dip

them in a container filled with hot water and then dry them with a clean cloth.

Desserts that need to be served warm can be made ahead and transferred into chafing dishes or warming trays placed over hot water baths.

10   What about flowers?

Whether you use flowers from a florist or fresh from the garden, flowers add tremendously to the atmosphere and to the overall appearance of your party.

Many flowers are available all year long. However, their availability and cost vary in different regions of the country. Talk to your florist about the best flower buys. For example, prices go up around major "flower" holidays—Christmas, Valentine's Day, and Mother's Day. Around these dates wholesale prices go up as much as 300%, and the cost is passed on to the consumer. In general, don't expect good prices or a great selection two weeks before to one week after these holidays. Before purchasing flowers for a party, consider:
- The table size
- Are the flowers to be used as a centerpiece or to add color to the food?
- How much food will be on the table? Make sure there is enough room for the desserts and the people before worrying about flowers.
- Do the flowers complement the food, serving pieces, linens, and party theme?
- Your party budget
- Fragrance. Avoid overpowering floral fragrances that might compete with the food.
- Make sure that flowers that will be used as a garnish or may have direct contact with food are *not* poisonous. Call your local poison control center for a complete list of poisonous flowers.

Your Party Countdown Calendar

Details, details, details: how does it all come together?
It is never too early to start planning a party. The following information can be used as a checklist as you count down to the day of your party.

1 Month Ahead
Mail invitations for formal parties and parties during the holidays.
Plan menu.
Write out menu timetable.
Write out party timetable.
Write out supply list.

2 Weeks Ahead
Contact guests who did not R.S.V.P.
Mail or telephone invitations for casual parties.
Order flowers.
Order rental equipment, if necessary.
Order wine.

1 Week Ahead
Do major housecleaning.
Clean linens.
Buy mineral and sparkling waters, paper products, and any special table settings.

3 Days Ahead
Do minor housecleaning.
Shop for all food items not already prepared.

The Day Before
Arrange and set tables.
Buy perishable foods.
Finish preparing desserts.
Chill wines.
Buy ice if beverages are not being delivered chilled.
Re-check menu timetable, party timetable, and supply list.
Thaw frozen desserts.
Deliveries.

The Party Day
Garnish desserts.
Arrange desserts on table.
Set up bar.
Have chilled wine and beverages delivered.
Have a dress rehearsal with any hired help.
Tidy house.
Clean kitchen.
Absolutely nothing should be left to be done when guests arrive.
Save at least 1 to 2 hours for yourself to relax before guests arrive.

2 Key Ingredients

Freshness, accurate measuring, and proper preparation of essential ingredients are vital factors in the successful outcome of a recipe. Before attempting any recipe, always read the recipe twice.

Butter

Unless shortening is specified, use butter. In general, margarine can be substituted for butter, but the flavor of the end product will not be as rich as it could be. Do not substitute whipped butter or light or diet margarine in these recipes because of the difference in volume and water content. There are two types of butter, salted and unsalted. For best results, use the type specified in each recipe.

Chocolate

There are several major types of chocolate: unsweetened, semi- or bittersweet, sweet chocolate, milk chocolate, and unsweetened cocoa powder. The percentage of chocolate liqueur, along with the amount of cocoa butter and sweetener, determines the type of chocolate. The combinations vary from manufacturer to manufacturer, and this gives the different brands of chocolate their own distinctive tastes.

White chocolate is not a real chocolate because it contains no chocolate liqueur; it is made of cocoa butter and sweetener.

Eggs

All the recipes in this book were tested with large eggs. When using eggs, make sure they are fresh and un-cracked. It is easier to separate eggs when they are cold. For greater volume, beat egg whites when they are at room temperature.

Flour

There are three types of flour used in this book: bread flour, all-purpose flour, and cake flour. These flours vary in the amount of gluten present in them, bread flour having the highest gluten content, and cake flour having the least. Gluten affects such things as dough elasticity and texture. For best results, use the specific type and amount of flour called for in a recipe's ingredients list.

Fruit

Fruit in season is at its peak of flavor and texture. Through the miracle of modern shipping, a wide variety of fruits from all over the country and world are available all year long. Most of the menus included in this book take advantage of seasonal fruits. Seek out top quality fruit to make these desserts and you will be rewarded with superlative finished products.

Nuts

Nuts add a taste all their own to desserts and baked goods. Following are ways of preparing nuts called for in this book:

Blanching Almonds: To blanch almonds, place them in a saucepan of boiling water for 1 minute, stirring constantly. Drain almonds, and rinse them in cold water. Gently squeeze almonds out of their skins. Dry almonds thoroughly before using in a recipe.

Skinning Hazelnuts: To skin hazelnuts, place them on a jelly roll pan and bake in a preheated 350° oven for 15 minutes or until their skins begin to parch and flake off. Transfer hazelnuts to waxed paper; cool completely. Rub hazelnuts between clean coarse kitchen towels until most of the skins are removed. Pick out the nuts, and discard the skins. (A few bits of skin may adhere to hazelnuts.)

Toasting Nuts: Toss nuts in a plastic bag with 1 teaspoon oil per 1 cup of nuts. Place lightly oiled nuts on a jelly roll pan. Toast in a preheated 300° oven for 10 to 15 minutes, stirring occasionally to ensure even browning.

3 Dessert Cheeses

Dessert buffets need a balance of sweet and savory flavors. There are hundreds of cheeses available today, and almost any can be a savory addition to your dessert menu. To serve cheese elegantly, aim for variety in taste, texture, and appearance. For best flavor, serve all cheeses at room temperature. There are many classifications of cheeses. Listed below are ones that work particularly well with desserts.

Soft-Ripening Cheeses

Triple cremes contain 75% butterfat. These cheeses are rich, smooth, luscious, and elegant. Basic triple cremes are Boursault, St. Andre, Brillat Savarin, and Explorateur. Mascarpone is an Italian fresh cheese which can be purchased plain or in tortes layered with pine nuts, basil, or Gorgonzola. Triple creme blues include Cambozola from Germany and Blue Castello from Denmark (also known as Danish Blue).

Fromage de chèvres (*goat cheeses*) are great summer cheeses. It is very important to taste these cheeses before buying them. French chèvres such as Montrachet and Pyramide are mild and easy to enjoy. These cheeses are highly perishable, so they should be eaten soon after purchasing. Fresh goat cheese means cheese that hasn't aged; it will be soft, wet, and mild. Aged goat cheeses are crumbly, dry, and tart. Chèvres are available in all shapes and sizes. They should be wrapped in wax paper rather than plastic so that they can breathe.

Double cremes contain 60 to 62% butterfat, resulting in a cheese that tastes like butter or heavy cream. There are many varieties of these soft-ripening cheeses; Brie and Camembert are the most famous. Camembert is a young cheese that has a stronger flavor than Brie.

Mountain Cheeses

Mountain cheeses are not as rich as cremes, but their flavors can stand alone. Doux de Montage ("sweet of the mountains") is a semi-firm French mountain cheese. Its flavor is rich but mild, similar to Havarti. Extra-Aged Gouda is a firm but tender, full-flavored cheese. As Goudas age they become harder, drier, and more flavorful.

Cheddars

Cheddar used as a dessert is an adventuresome way to entertain. Cheddars must be served with fresh fruits (i.e., pears, apples, and grapes) to help offset the saltiness of the cheese. England and the United States both produce excellent cheddar cheeses. English white cheddars such as Caerphilly and Dunlop have a mild, buttermilk-like taste. Sharp American cheeses have a combination of sulphur and salt flavor. Serve only sharp cheddars with fruit since cheeses such as Colby just don't have enough flavor. If possible, try to have your wedge of cheddar cut from a whole wheel rather than getting a precut, prewrapped portion. For a good color/flavor combination, serve one American cheddar and one English cheddar with slices of fresh fruit and wheatmeal crackers.

Blue-veined Cheeses

A blue-veined cheese served with fruit and port is a very traditional dessert. Examples of blue-veined cheeses are Stilton from England, Gorgonzola from Italy, Maytag Blue from Iowa, Oregon Blue, and Rougefort from France. These cheeses work best by themselves and should not be mixed with other blue-veined cheeses. Serve blue-veined cheeses with rich, bland crackers, walnuts, and honeyed or glazed fruits.

4

Pretty Spring Parties

Mid-Morning Muffin Break
Caribbean Anniversary Romantique
A Charity Auction Dessert Brunch
Elegant Easter Brunch
Fiesta Cinco de Mayo
A Bridesmaids' Tea

Mid-Morning Muffin Break

Poppy Seed Muffins
Almond Fudge Brownie Muffins
Honey-Glazed Bran Muffins
Blueberry Streusel Muffins
Orange Date-Nut Muffins
Whipped Honey Butter
Citrus Spread
Assorted Fresh Fruit
Assorted Fruit Preserves

Muffins are a classic comfort food. They have been favorites at the American table for centuries. Sensationally versatile, simple to prepare, inexpensive, and easy to transport, homemade muffins require minimal effort for maximum enjoyment.

A mid-morning muffin break is perfect for staff meetings or office celebrations—a cheery energizer before everyone gets down to business.

This party is ideal for people too busy to spend a lot of time preparing food and decorating. Colorful paper and plastic tablecloths, napkins, plates, cups, and utensils will transform a conference room or employee lounge into a festive buffet. Contrast paper and plastic tableware with baskets filled with muffins and fruit. Bring a special coffee blend and let the office coffeepot provide the brew. What a pleasant way to start the business day!

Poppy Seed Muffins, Almond Fudge Brownie Muffins, Blueberry Streusel Muffins, and Orange Date-Nut Muffins with Whipped Honey Butter and Citrus Spread

Poppy Seed Muffins

Poppy seeds are the dried seeds of the opium poppy flower native to the Middle East. They add a subtle nutty taste to these moist muffins.
Makes 1 dozen.

2 cups all-purpose flour
2½ tablespoons poppy seeds
1 teaspoon baking powder
½ teaspoon salt
½ teaspoon baking soda
¾ cup granulated sugar
½ cup unsalted butter, softened
2 eggs
¾ cup sour cream
½ teaspoon almond extract

Line 12 standard muffin tins with paper bake cups; set aside. Preheat oven to 375°. Stir together flour, poppy seeds, baking powder, salt, and baking soda in a bowl; set aside. Beat sugar and butter in a medium bowl on medium speed until light and fluffy. Add eggs, one at a time, beating well after each addition. Beat in sour cream and almond extract. Add dry ingredients to egg mixture, stirring until just moistened. Fill prepared muffin tins two-thirds full. Bake for 20 minutes or until a cake tester inserted in center comes out clean. Cool in tins for 5 minutes; turn muffins out onto wire rack. Serve warm or cool.

Almond Fudge Brownie Muffins

Makes 1 dozen.

¾ cup semi-sweet chocolate chips
2 1-ounce squares unsweetened chocolate, coarsely chopped
⅓ cup unsalted butter
¾ cup sour cream
⅔ cup firmly packed brown sugar
¼ cup light corn syrup
1 egg
1¼ teaspoons vanilla
1½ cups all-purpose flour
1 teaspoon baking soda
¼ teaspoon salt
1 cup semi-sweet chocolate chips
½ cup slivered almonds

Line twelve muffin tins with paper bake cups; set aside. Preheat oven to 400°. Melt ¾ cup semi-sweet chocolate chips, unsweetened chocolate, and butter in top of a double boiler set over simmering water, stirring until smooth. Remove from heat. Cool for 5 minutes. Whisk sour cream, brown sugar, corn syrup, egg, and vanilla into chocolate mixture.
Stir together flour, baking soda, and salt in a large bowl. Add 1 cup chocolate chips. Add chocolate mixture to dry ingredients; stir until just moistened. Fill prepared muffin tins three-quarters full; sprinkle with slivered almonds. Bake for 20 minutes or until a cake tester inserted in center comes out almost clean. Cool in tins for 5 minutes; turn out onto a wire rack. Serve warm or cool.

Honey-Glazed Bran Muffins

This traditional bran muffin batter is poured into honey-lined muffin tins to give a new twist to an old favorite.
Makes 1 dozen.

Honey Glaze
    2 tablespoons unsalted butter
    3 tablespoons firmly packed brown sugar
    3 tablespoons granulated sugar
    1 tablespoon honey
    1½ teaspoons water

Muffins
    1 cup whole wheat flour, sifted
    1 cup unprocessed bran flakes
    ½ cup golden raisins
    ½ cup chopped pecans
    2 teaspoons baking powder
    2 teaspoons baking soda
    ½ teaspoon salt
    1 egg, beaten
    1 cup milk
    3 tablespoons vegetable oil
    2 tablespoons honey
    2 tablespoons molasses
    1 teaspoon apple cider vinegar

For glaze, beat butter in a small mixing bowl until light and fluffy. Gradually beat in brown sugar and granulated sugar. Beat in 1 tablespoon honey and water until fluffy. Liberally coat bottom and sides of 12 muffin tins with honey glaze; set aside.

Preheat oven to 425°. For muffins, stir together whole wheat flour, bran flakes, raisins, pecans, baking powder, baking soda, and salt in a large bowl. Combine beaten egg, milk, oil, 2 tablespoons honey, molasses, and cider vinegar in a small bowl. Add egg mixture to dry ingredients; stir until just moistened. Fill prepared muffin tins two-thirds full. Bake for 15 to 20 minutes or until a cake tester inserted in center comes out clean. Immediately turn muffins out onto wire rack. Serve warm or cool.

Blueberry Streusel Muffins

If you substitute frozen blueberries for fresh, make certain they are still frozen or only partially thawed. Fully defrosted berries may break down while baking and make the muffins soggy.
Makes 1 dozen.

Streusel Topping
    ¼ cup all-purpose flour, sifted
    ¼ cup granulated sugar
    ½ teaspoon ground cinnamon
    2 tablespoons unsalted butter, softened

Muffins
    ½ cup unsalted butter, softened
    1 cup granulated sugar
    3 eggs
    1 cup sour cream
    1 teaspoon vanilla
    2 cups all-purpose flour
    1 teaspoon baking soda
    ½ teaspoon salt
    2 cups fresh or frozen blueberries, partially thawed and
      drained

For topping, stir together ¼ cup flour, ¼ cup sugar, and cinnamon in a small bowl. Cut in butter with a pastry blender or fork until mixture resembles crumbs; set aside.

Line 12 muffin tins with paper bake cups; set aside. Preheat oven to 350°. For muffins, cream ½ cup butter and 1 cup sugar in a large mixing bowl on medium-high speed until light and fluffy. Add eggs, one at a time, blending well after each addition. Blend in sour cream and vanilla. Stir together 2 cups of flour, baking soda, and salt in a bowl. Add dry ingredients to butter mixture; stir until just moistened. Fold in blueberries. Fill prepared muffin tins two-thirds full; sprinkle each with streusel topping. Bake 15 to 20 minutes, or until a cake tester inserted in center comes out clean. Cool in tins for 5 minutes; turn muffins out onto a wire rack. Serve warm or cool.

Orange Date-Nut Muffins

The aroma of these muffins baking is surpassed only by their flavor.
Makes 1 dozen.

2 cups all-purpose flour
⅔ cup granulated sugar
1 tablespoon baking powder
1 cup chopped dates
1 cup chopped walnuts
4½ teaspoons finely grated orange peel
⅔ cup fresh orange juice
⅓ cup butter, melted
1 egg

Orange Glaze
½ cup confectioners' sugar, sifted
2 to 3 teaspoons fresh orange juice
1½ teaspoons grated orange peel

Line 12 muffin tins with paper bake cups; set aside. Preheat oven to 400°. Stir together flour (reserve 2 tablespoons flour), sugar, and baking powder in a large bowl. Combine dates, walnuts, 4½ teaspoons orange peel, and reserved flour in a small bowl. Combine ⅔ cup orange juice, melted butter, and egg in a small bowl. Stir orange juice mixture into flour mixture; stir until just moistened. Fold in date mixture. Fill prepared muffin tins two-thirds full. Bake for 20 minutes or until cake tester inserted in center comes out clean. Cool in pans for 5 minutes; turn muffins out onto a wire rack.

Meanwhile, for glaze, beat together sifted confectioners' sugar, 2 teaspoons orange juice, and 1½ teaspoons orange peel in a small bowl until smooth. Stir in additional orange juice to make glaze spreading consistency. Spread glaze over warm muffins; allow to set. Serve warm or cool.

Note: Unglazed Orange Date-Nut Muffins freeze well for up to 3 months. To freeze, completely cool muffins; wrap first in plastic wrap and then in aluminum foil. Defrost muffins at room temperature. Spread glaze over defrosted muffins.

Whipped Honey Butter

Delicious spread on hot biscuits, muffins, toast, or scones, this honey-kissed spread will keep in the refrigerator for about 1 week.
Makes ¾ cup.

½ cup unsalted butter, softened
¼ cup honey

Beat together butter and honey in a small mixing bowl on medium-high speed until smooth. Cover and refrigerate until ready to serve. Serve at room temperature.

Citrus Spread

Makes about 1 cup.

4 ounces cream cheese, softened
3 tablespoons butter, softened
2 tablespoons orange juice
1 to 2 tablespoons honey
1 tablespoon grated orange peel
1 teaspoon lemon juice

Combine cream cheese, butter, orange juice, 1 tablespoon honey, orange peel, and lemon juice in a small mixing bowl on medium speed until smooth. Add additional honey to taste, if desired. Cover and refrigerate until ready to serve.

Note: Citrus spread can be prepared 1 week in advance.

Caribbean Anniversary Romantique

Triple Layer Toasted Coconut Cake
Key Lime Mousse
Gingered Pineapple
Papaya Fans with Macadamias and Lime
Banana Daquiri Slush

Whether celebrating a first, tenth, twenty-fifth, or fiftieth wedding anniversary, this light, refreshing island banquet will bring back memories of a honeymoon in the Caribbean, South Pacific, or Hawaii.

Recreate a fresh, sun-kissed atmosphere by coordinating the colors of the Caribbean's white sandy beaches, clear blue skies, turquoise sea, and pink coral reefs in your table coverings, platters, glasswares, and accent pieces. Sea shells and other marine motifs add to the festivity.

From Jamaica to Barbados, influences from the French, Portuguese, Spanish, and English combined with the Caribbean's tropical bounty of bananas, coconuts, mangoes, papayas, limes, pineapple, coffee, sugar cane, and ginger are found in cakes, pies, tarts, and beverages. The exotic flavors of the Caribbean are showcased in this collection of luscious desserts. Triple Layer Toasted Coconut Cake, Papaya Fans with Macadamia Nuts, and Key Lime Mousse are but a few of the many special desserts offered in this party menu. Instead of champagne, toast the couple with Banana Daquiri Slush, made with the Caribbean's official beverage, rum.

Triple Layer Toasted Coconut Cake

Coconut milk is made by pressing a mixture of shredded coconut and hot water through a sieve. After the milk rests, it separates into two layers. The thick layer is coconut cream. For use in desserts a sweetener is added, yielding cream of coconut. Cream of coconut is available canned or frozen in most grocery stores and liquor stores. If unavailable, substitute half and half.

Serves 10.

Cake
3 cups cake flour, sifted
1 tablespoon baking powder
1 cup unsalted butter, softened
2 cups granulated sugar
1 teaspoon vanilla
4 egg yolks, at room temperature
¾ cup milk
¼ cup cream of coconut
6 egg whites, at room temperature
¼ teaspoon salt

Toasted Coconut Buttercream
1 cup unsalted butter, softened
2½ cups confectioners' sugar, sifted
1 egg yolk, at room temperature
2 tablespoons Grand Marnier
1 teaspoon orange juice concentrate
1 cup shredded coconut, toasted

Garnish
½ cup shredded coconut, toasted

For cake, lightly butter three 8- or 9-inch cake pans. Line bottom of each pan with a circle of waxed paper. Dust sides of the pans with flour; set aside. Preheat oven to 350°. Stir together flour and baking powder in a bowl. Beat 1 cup butter in a medium mixing bowl on medium speed until smooth. Gradually beat in granulated sugar and vanilla; beat until light and fluffy. Add 4 egg yolks, one at a time, beating well after each addition. Combine milk and cream of coconut

in a small bowl. Alternately add flour mixture and milk mixture to sugar mixture, beating on low speed till well combined, beginning and ending with flour. Set aside.

Beat egg whites and salt in a large mixing bowl on medium speed until frothy. Increase speed to high and beat until stiff. Gently fold egg whites, one third at a time, into batter. Gently pour batter into prepared pans; smooth tops. Bake for 30 to 35 minutes or until a cake tester inserted in center comes out clean. Cool in pans for 10 minutes; turn cakes out onto wire racks. Peel off waxed paper. Invert cakes onto another wire rack so that the layers are right side up. Cool completely.

For buttercream, beat 1 cup butter in a large mixing bowl on medium speed until light. Gradually and confectioners' sugar to butter, beating until light and fluffy. Add egg yolk; beat well. Add Grand Marnier and orange juice concentrate to butter mixture; beat till well combined. Gently fold 1 cup toasted coconut into buttercream.

To assemble, place one cake layer on a serving plate. Spread with about ¼ cup buttercream. Top with second cake layer. Repeat procedure ending with third cake layer. Frost tops and sides of cake with remaining buttercream. Sprinkle top with ½ cup toasted coconut.

Tip: To toast coconut, preheat oven to 350°. Evenly spread coconut on a baking sheet. Bake for 10 to 12 minutes or until golden brown.

Triple Layer Toasted Coconut Cake, Key Lime Mousse, Papaya Fans with Macadamias and Lime, and Banana Daquiri Slush

Key Lime Mousse

If Florida Key limes are not available, substitute Persian limes which are readily available in your supermarket produce section.
Serves 10 to 12.

⅓ cup plus 3 tablespoons fresh Key lime juice
1 teaspoon finely grated Key lime peel
1 envelope unflavored gelatin
1 cup whipping cream
6 egg whites, at room temperature
¼ teaspoon salt
3 cups confectioners' sugar, sifted
½ cup unsalted butter, softened
6 egg yolks, at room temperature
2 tablespoons coarsely grated lime peel (optional)

In top of a double boiler, stir together lime juice and 1 teaspoon lime peel. Sprinkle gelatin over lime mixture and set aside for 10 minutes to soften. Place double boiler over low heat and stir lime mixture until gelatin dissolves. Remove from heat and let mixture cool to room temperature.

Beat whipping cream in a chilled bowl with chilled beaters until stiff. Cover and refrigerate until ready to use.

Beat egg whites and salt in a medium mixing bowl on medium-high speed until soft peaks form. Gradually add 1 cup confectioners' sugar and beat until stiff; set aside.

Beat butter in a large mixing bowl on medium speed until soft and fluffy. Add 1 cup confectioners' sugar; beat until smooth. Add egg yolks, one at a time, beating well after each addition. Alternately add dissolved gelatin and 1 cup confectioners' sugar; beat until smooth. Fold in egg whites, one-third at a time. Fold in whipped cream. Turn mousse into a serving dish. Cover and refrigerate until chilled and set, about 3 hours. Garnish with 2 tablespoons lime peel, if desired.

Gingered Pineapple

Serves 6.

1 cup sour cream
¼ cup honey
3 tablespoons finely chopped crystalized ginger
1 large fresh pineapple

Stir together sour cream and honey in a small bowl. Stir in crystalized ginger; set aside.

Cut pineapple from the bottom through the crown, first in half, then in quarters. Cut away the core strip, leaving the crown on. Loosen fruit by cutting close to the shell with a thin sharp knife. Cut loosened fruit crosswise, then cut lengthwise once or twice to make bite-sized pieces. Leave pineapple in shell or place in a serving bowl. Spoon ginger mixture over pineapple. Refrigerate until ready to serve. Serve cool or at room temperature.

Papaya Fans with Macadamias and Lime

Serves 8.

4 large ripe papayas
Peel of 2 limes, finely grated
½ cup dark rum
1 cup coarsely chopped macadamia nuts, toasted
2 limes, quartered

Peel papayas and halve lengthwise; discard seeds. Slice papayas lengthwise, starting from wide end and slicing almost to the narrow end; fan slices out on 8 serving plates. Sprinkle some of the lime peel and 1½ to 3 teaspoons rum over each serving. Chill.

To serve, sprinkle macadamia nuts over papayas. Garnish with lime wedges.

Banana Daquiri Slush

Serves 8.

1 cup light rum
½ cup fresh lime juice
½ cup banana liqueur
4 medium ripe bananas, sliced
2½ cups crushed ice
2 medium bananas, peeled and quartered lengthwise

Combine rum, lime juice, and banana liqueur in a blender. Cover and blend till smooth. Add bananas, one at a time; blend well. Add ice, blend until slushy. Pour into large serving glasses. Garnish with banana spears.

A Charity Auction Dessert Buffet

Mixed Berries on the Half Shell
Champagne Mousse Parfait
Chocolate Pâte with Pistachio Crème Anglaise
Raspberry Truffle Torte

Spring is the perfect season for a charity auction. With the season there comes a fever of renewed energies, an openness for giving, and a sense for change and growth. An auction is a special way to raise private donations for your favorite charity, whether for a children's hospital, crisis hot line, high-school band uniforms, or food bank. Attract and reward donors and guests with a dessert buffet—the perfect finale to an energetic evening of bidding.

Richness and elegance are the keys to this menu, and what could be more dramatic than chocolate, fresh berries, and champagne? Complement these desserts in a table set with your best linens, china, crystal, and silver.

Mixed Berries on the Half Shell

24

Mixed Berries on the Half Shell

Delicate cookie shells cradle orange scented cream and assorted fresh berries.
Serves 8.

Pâte Sable
  For recipe, see page 000.
Filling
  1 cup whipping cream
  1 3-ounce package cream cheese, softened
  ½ cup granulated sugar
  1 tablespoon orange peel
  1 tablespoon fresh orange juice
  ⅓ cup seedless raspberry preserves
  2 tablespoons Grand Marnier
  2 pints assorted fresh berries, rinsed and stemmed
    (strawberries, raspberries, or blueberries)

Prepare Pâte Sable as directed. Preheat oven to 350°.
Divide dough into 12 equal pieces. Roll each piece out to a
4-inch circle, ⅛-inch thick on a lightly floured surface. Press
each round onto the back of an ungreased 4-inch scallop
shell. Pierce dough all over with fork. Repeat with remaining
pastry. Arrange shells, pastry side up, on a baking sheet. Bake
for 12 to 15 minutes or until light brown. Immediately remove pastry from back of shell and gently transfer pastry inside of shell. Cool completely.

For filling, beat whipping cream in a chilled bowl with
chilled beaters until soft peaks form. Beat in cream cheese.
Gradually beat in sugar. Stir in orange peel and orange juice.
Refrigerate until ready to use.

Heat respberry preserves in a small heat-proof cup over
medium heat, stirring until thin. Remove from heat; stir in
Grand Marnier.

To assemble, fill each pastry shell with a dollop of cream
cheese filling. Arrange berries on top. Brush berries with preserve mixture. Serve immediately.

Champagne Mousse Parfait

Serves 8.

  8 egg yolks, at room temperature
  ½ cup granulated sugar
  Pinch of salt
  1 cup champagne
  1 cup whipping cream
  8 egg whites, at room temperature
  16 fresh strawberries, rinsed, stemmed, and sliced
  8 whole strawberries, rinsed with stem intact

Beat egg yolks, sugar, and salt in a mixing bowl on high
speed until pale yellow. Transfer yolk mixture to the top of a
double boiler set over simmering water. Gradually whisk in
champagne. Continue whisking until mixture triples in volume and holds soft peaks, about 5 minutes. Remove from
heat. Transfer mixture to a large bowl. Cool in refrigerator;
stir occasionally.

Meanwhile, beat whipping cream in a chilled bowl with
chilled beaters until stiff; set aside. Beat egg whites in a clean,
dry bowl with clean dry beaters until stiff. Gently fold whipped cream into egg yolk mixture. Gently fold egg whites, one
third at a time, into mixture. Spoon mixture, alternating with
layers of sliced strawberries, into champagne flutes. Top each
serving with a whole strawberry. Chill until set, about 2
hours.

Chocolate Pâte with Pistachio Crème Anglaise

Simple chocolate bliss!
Serves 12 to 15.

1½ cups unsalted butter
1⅓ cups semi-sweet chocolate chips
4 1-ounce squares unsweetened chocolate, coarsely
  chopped
2 cups unsweetened cocoa powder, preferably Dutch
  process
⅔ cup granulated sugar
½ cup water
2 eggs
4 egg yolks
2 tablespoons vanilla
Pinch of salt

Butter an 8½ × 4½ × 2¾-inch loaf pan. Line the bottom with parchment paper. Melt butter, semi-sweet chocolate, and unsweetened chocolate in top of a double boiler set over simmering water, stirring until smooth. Stir in cocoa powder. Remove from heat.

Combine ⅔ cup sugar and water in a small saucepan over medium-low heat, stirring until sugar dissolves. Remove from heat. Cool completely. Stir cooled sugar mixture into chocolate mixture. Beat eggs, 4 egg yolks, vanilla, and salt in a large bowl. Whisk chocolate mixture into egg mixture. Pour into prepared loaf pan; cover with plastic wrap. Refrigerate overnight.

Prepare Pistachio Crème Anglaise as directed.

To serve, loosen pâte by partially submerging loaf pan in hot water for about 30 to 45 seconds. Invert pâte onto a serving platter. Peel off parchment paper. Cut pâte into slices using a hot, dry knife. Spoon chilled Pistachio Crème Anglaise onto serving dishes; top with a slice of pâte. Sprinkle with additional pistachios, if desired.

Raspberry Truffle Torte

This is a rich chocolate dessert that also makes a fabulous end to an important meal.
Serves 12.

Genoise
6 eggs, at room temperature
1 cup granulated sugar
1 teaspoon vanilla
½ cup plus 2 tablespoons unsalted butter, melted
½ cup all-purpose flour
½ cup unsweetened cocoa powder, preferably Dutch
   process

Syrup
¾ cup granulated sugar
1 cup water
⅓ cup framboise

Ganache
2 cups whipping cream
12 ounces bittersweet chocolate, chopped
¼ cup framboise
¼ cup sifted unsweetened cocoa powder, preferably Dutch
   process

Icing
½ cup unsalted butter, softened
1 cup confectioners' sugar, sifted
⅔ cup unsweetened cocoa powder, preferably Dutch
   process
2 to 3 tablespoons milk
2 tablespoons framboise
1 teaspoon vanilla
2 cups plus 12 fresh raspberries

Grease and flour three 8-inch round cake pans. Preheat oven to 350°. Beat eggs in a medium mixing bowl until light in color, about 5 minutes. Gradually beat in 1 cup granulated sugar. Stir in 1 teaspoon vanilla and melted butter. Sift together flour and ½ cup cocoa powder in a small bowl. Gently fold cocoa mixture into egg mixture. Gently pour mixture evenly into prepared pans. Bake for 12 to 15 minutes or until top springs back when lightly touched in center. Cool 5 minutes. Remove cakes from pans and cool completely on wire racks.

Meanwhile, for syrup, combine ¾ cup granulated sugar and water in a small, heavy saucepan over medium heat, stirring constantly until sugar dissolves. Bring to a boil and boil for 5 minutes. Remove from heat. Cool syrup to room temperature. Stir in ⅓ cup framboise. Prick cake layers with a fork; pour syrup evenly over each layer.

For ganache, place whipping cream in a medium, heavy saucepan set over medium-low heat; scald. Do not boil. Remove from heat. Add chocolate and whisk until melted. Stir in ¼ cup framboise. Pour mixture into a bowl, stirring occasionally until cool. Cover bowl; chill completely. Remove 1 cup of ganache. Working quickly to prevent melting, shape mixture into 12 small balls. Place ¼ cup cocoa powder in a shallow dish. Roll balls in cocoa powder. Refrigerate in an airtight container until ready to use.

For icing, beat butter in a medium mixing bowl on medium speed until light and fluffy. Sift together confectioners' sugar and ⅔ cup cocoa powder in a small bowl. Gradually add sugar mixture to butter; beat until smooth. Add 2 tablespoons milk, 2 tablespoons framboise, and 1 teaspoon vanilla; blend well. Add additional milk, if necessary, to make icing of spreading consistency.

To assemble, place one genoise layer on a serving platter, pricked side up. Spread 1 cup ganache over layer. Arrange 1 cup raspberries over ganache. Top with second genoise layer. Cover with 1 cup ganache, then 1 cup raspberries. Top with remaining genoise layer. Spread icing evenly over top layer. Decorate cake with truffles and remaining raspberries. Refrigerate until ready to serve.

Elegant Easter Brunch

Hot Cross Buns
Popovers Filled with Spring Herb Scramble
Champagne Poppy Seed Fruit Salad
Chocolate Mousse Eggs with Framboise Sauce
Champagne Magnolia

With Easter the long, cold winter ends and a new, rejuvenating spring begins. This fresh Easter brunch is perfect for a special holiday gathering with family and friends. There are a number of ways you can bring the colors of spring to your holiday table. Begin by decorating your table with linens and ceramic serving pieces in the pastel hues of the season. Fresh tulips and daffodils along with brightly colored Easter eggs make the perfect backdrop. Start your celebration by greeting guests with long glass flutes filled with eye-opening Champagne Magnolia.

Hot Cross Buns

For centuries Hot Cross Buns have been traditional Easter fare in England. This version will rise to the occasion. *Makes 2 dozen.*

1 cup milk
1 package active dry yeast
¼ cup warm water (105° to 115°)
⅓ cup granulated sugar
⅓ cup unsalted butter, softened
2 tablespoons light brown sugar
2 eggs
1 teaspoon ground cinnamon
½ teaspoon ground nutmeg
¼ teaspoon ground cloves
Dash of salt
3½ to 4½ cups bread or all-purpose flour
½ cup dried currants

Glaze
1 egg white, lightly beaten
1 tablespoon water

Icing
1½ cups confectioners' sugar, sifted
1 tablespoon unsalted butter, softened
1 tablespoon fresh lemon juice
2 to 3 teaspoons milk

Generously grease a large bowl; set aside. Scald milk in a heavy, 2-quart saucepan over medium heat. Remove from heat, cool to room temperature. Dissolve yeast in warm water in a large mixing bowl. Beat in granulated sugar, ⅓ cup butter, brown sugar, eggs, cinnamon, nutmeg, cloves, and salt on low speed, blending well. Add 2 cups of the flour. Increase speed to medium and beat for 2 minutes. Stir in 1 cup flour. Stir in currants. Turn dough out onto a floured surface and knead about 5 minutes or until smooth and elastic. Shape dough into a ball and place in greased bowl; turn once to grease top. Cover and let rise in a warm, draft-free place until double, about 1½ hours.

Grease two baking sheets. Punch dough down. Divide dough into 4 equal parts. Cut each quarter into 6 equal pieces. Shape each piece into a ball; place about 2 inches apart on prepared baking sheets. Snip a cross on top of each ball with scissors. Cover and let rise in a warm, draft-free place until double, about 1 hour.

Preheat oven to 350°. For glaze, beat egg white and water in a cup. Brush tops of buns with egg white mixture using a pastry brush. Bake for 15 to 20 minutes or until golden brown. Cool buns completely on a wire rack.

Meanwhile, for icing, beat together confectioners' sugar, 1 tablespoon butter, lemon juice, and 2 teaspoons milk in a bowl until smooth. Add additional milk, if necessary, to make an icing of spreading consistency. Fill a pastry bag fitted with a small round plain tip with icing. Pipe icing to form a cross on each bun using cuts as a guide.

Popovers Filled with Spring Herb Scramble, Hot Cross Buns, Chocolate Mousse Eggs with Framboise Sauce, and Champagne Magnolia

Popovers Filled with Spring Herb Scramble

Serves 8.

Popovers
  6 eggs
  2 cups milk
  2 cups all-purpose flour
  ¾ teaspoon salt
  6 tablespoons unsalted butter

Filling
  16 eggs
  ⅓ cup whipping cream
  4 tablespoons unsalted butter
  ⅓ cup chopped fresh spring herbs (dill, rosemary, or tarragon)
  ¼ cup finely chopped green onions
  Salt and pepper, to taste

For popovers, generously grease 8 popover pan cups or custard cups; place on a baking sheet. Preheat oven to 400°. Beat 6 eggs in a bowl. Add milk; beat until blended. Set aside. Combine flour and salt in a bowl. Cut in 6 tablespoons butter using a pastry blender or two knives scissor-fashion until mixture resembles coarse crumbs. Gradually add flour mixture to egg mixture; blend well. Fill prepared popover cups three-quarters full with batter. Bake for 1 hour or until golden brown. Remove popovers from cups.

Meanwhile, prepare egg filling. Whisk 16 eggs and whipping cream in a large bowl until blended. Melt 4 tablespoons butter in a large, heavy skillet over low heat. Add egg mixture and cook, stirring constantly with a wooden spoon, scraping sides and bottom of pan, until eggs begin to thicken and tiny curds form, about 20 to 25 minutes. Add herbs and green onions. Cook until eggs are soft and creamy. Do not overcook eggs. Remove from heat. Season with salt and pepper.

To assemble, cut tops off popovers and remove any moist batter remaining in center. Spoon egg mixture into popovers until completely full; replace top. Serve immediately.

Variation: Add ½ to 1 cup chopped smoked salmon to egg mixture.

Note: To season popover pan, grease cups and place in a preheated 400° oven for 30 minutes. Remove remaining grease. Regrease cups before using.

Champagne Poppy Seed Fruit Salad

You can buy champagne vinegar in most specialty food stores or use rice wine vinegar instead.
Serves 8.

  2 tablespoons dry white wine
  1 tablespoon dry mustard
  ¾ cup granulated sugar
  ⅓ cup champagne vinegar
  1 tablespoon poppy seeds
  1 teaspoon salt
  ¼ teaspoon white pepper
  ½ cup vegetable oil
  ½ cup olive oil
  Assorted fresh seasonal fruits, washed and cut into bite-sized pieces

Whisk together wine and mustard in a medium bowl; let stand for 10 minutes. Add sugar, vinegar, poppy seeds, salt, and white pepper to wine mixture, whisking well to combine ingredients and dissolve sugar. Combine vegetable oil and olive oil in a small bowl. Slowly pour oils into poppy seed mixture, whisking constantly until oils are absorbed and dressing is thickened. Refrigerate, tightly covered, until ready to use.

Toss together assorted fruits in a salad bowl. Just before serving, pour desired amount of salad dressing over fruit; gently toss until fruit is covered with dressing.

Note: Champagne Poppy Seed Dressing can be made up to 5 days in advance.

Chocolate Mousse Eggs with Framboise Sauce

Chocolate and eggs are synonymous with Easter. These chocolate mousse eggs nestled in a pool of raspberry sauce are sure to become a traditional part of your Easter dinner or brunch menu.
Serves 8.

Mousse
1⅓ cups semi-sweet chocolate chips
½ cup unsalted butter, cut into pieces
2 tablespoons water
¼ cup confectioners' sugar
6 egg yolks, beaten
1 tablespoon dark rum
½ teaspoon vanilla
6 egg whites, at room temperature
2 tablespoons granulated sugar

Framboise Sauce
1 pound fresh, rinsed raspberries
⅓ cup granulated sugar
1 tablespoon framboise

For mousse, melt chocolate, butter, and water in top of a double boiler set over simmering water, stirring until smooth. Stir in confectioners' sugar. Slowly stir half of the chocolate mixture into beaten egg yolks. Stir egg mixture back into chocolate mixture in double boiler, blending well. Remove from heat. Stir in rum and vanilla; set aside. Beat egg whites in a large mixing bowl on high speed until foamy. Gradually add 2 tablespoons granulated sugar, beating until stiff. Gently fold chocolate mixture into beaten egg whites. Cover and refrigerate for at least 4 hours.

For Framboise Sauce, combine raspberries and ⅓ cup granulated sugar in a small, heavy saucepan. Cook over medium heat, stirring until sugar dissolves. Simmer until juices thicken slightly. Remove from heat. Strain mixture through a fine sieve into a small bowl. Stir in framboise. Cover and chill for at least 1 hour, or overnight.

To serve, spoon Framboise Sauce onto 8 individual serving plates. Using a tablespoon, scoop 2 rounded spoonfuls of mousse onto each plate. Serve immediately.

Champagne Magnolia

Serves 8.

16 tablespoons Grand Marnier
1 750-milliliter bottle brut champagne
2 cups freshly squeezed orange juice
8 fresh mint leaves (optional)

Add 2 tablespoons Grand Marnier to 8 champagne flutes. Pour champagne over liqueur until glass is two-thirds full. Top with orange juice. Garnish with mint leaves, if desired.

Fiesta Cinco de Mayo

Margarita Soufflé
Suspiros
Churros
Caramelized Flan with Cinnamon Sugar Tortillas
Fruit Gazpacho with Citrus Dressing
Cafe Mexicano

Cinco de Mayo marks the May 1862 victory of the Mexican army over the French forces of Maximillan and is celebrated as Independence Day in Mexico.

The Aztecs and Mayas had no butter, cream, or sugar. For dessert they relied on the vast assemblage of fruits that were available year round. After Mexico's conquest by Spain, however, the Spanish created intensely sweet desserts based primarily on sugar and eggs.

This menu combines traditional and contemporary desserts. Flan, probably the most popular of Mexican desserts, is caramelized and served with cinnamon sugar tortillas here. The flavors of lime and tequila, typical of the culture, are used in a frozen Margarita Soufflé. Recipes for Suspiros, Churros, and Fruit Gazpacho are also included. Serve any of these south of the border treats with Cafe Mexicano.

Set the scene for a Cinco de Mayo party by adorning the house with colorful decorations. Hang ribbons, crepe paper streamers, or garlands. Then climax the fiesta with the breaking of the piñata.

Suspiros, Caramelized Flan with Cinnamon Sugar Tortillas, Fruit Gazpacho with Citrus Dressing

Margarita Soufflé

This soufflé freezes well and needs only a quick garnishing before serving.
Serves 12.

2 envelopes unflavored gelatin
¼ cup triple sec
¼ cup tequila
10 egg yolks, at room temperature
1 cup granulated sugar
1 cup fresh lime juice
Peel of 4 limes, finely grated
2 teaspoons salt
10 egg whites, at room temperature
2 cups whipping cream

To make a collar for a 1½-quart soufflé dish, first tear a piece of aluminum foil 4 to 6 inches longer than the dish's circumference. Fold foil in half lengthwise. Fit foil around the outside of the soufflé dish, extending 3 inches above the top, and secure with a string tied 2 to 3 inches above the base of the dish or secure with tape. Set aside.

Sprinkle gelatin over triple sec and tequila in a small bowl; let stand for 5 minutes. Beat egg yolks in a medium mixing bowl until light and fluffy. Gradually add sugar, beating until smooth and light in color. Beat in lime juice, grated lime peel, and salt. Transfer mixture to top of a double boiler. Cook over simmering water, stirring constantly, until mixture thickens. Add triple sec mixture; stir until gelatin dissolves. Remove from heat. Cool completely.

Beat egg whites in a large mixing bowl on high speed, until stiff. Gently fold cooled yolk mixture into egg whites. Beat whipping cream in a chilled bowl with chilled beaters until stiff. Fold whipped cream into egg white mixture. Spoon mixture into prepared soufflé dish. Chill for 6 hours or overnight.

Note: Soufflé improves in flavor if made a day in advance.

Suspiros

Suspiros are delicate meringue cookies dusted with Mexican chocolate. If Mexican chocolate is unavailable in your area, you can substitute 2 ounces semi-sweet chocolate plus 1 teaspoon ground cinnamon.
Makes 3 dozen.

2 egg whites, at room temperature
⅛ teaspoon salt
¾ cup granulated sugar
2 ounces Mexican or semi-sweet chocolate, finely grated
½ teaspoon vanilla

Line baking sheets with parchment paper; set aside. Preheat oven to 350°. Beat egg whites and salt in a medium mixing bowl on high speed until foamy. Gradually add sugar, beating until stiff. Fold in chocolate and vanilla. Drop egg white mixture by tablespoonfuls 2 inches apart onto cookie sheets. Place cookie sheets in oven; immediately turn off heat. Let meringues sit in oven for 3 hours; do not open door. Remove from oven; tap cookie sheet bottoms lightly to loosen meringues. Cool on wire racks. Store in an airtight container at room temperature for up to 1 week.

Churros

Churros are a popular street food found throughout Mexico. These fried pastry puffs are best eaten warm.
Makes 2 dozen.

1½ cups water
½ cup unsalted butter
2 teaspoons grated lemon peel
2 teaspoons granulated sugar
1½ cups all-purpose flour, sifted
¼ teaspoon ground cardamom
¼ teaspoon salt
3 eggs, at room temperature
Vegetable oil for deep-fat frying
½ lime
¼ cup granulated sugar
2 teaspoons ground cinnamon

Combine water, butter, lemon peel, and 2 teaspoons sugar in a heavy, 2-quart saucepan over medium heat; bring to a boil. Stir in flour, cardamom, and salt. Immediately remove from heat. Beat mixture with an electric mixer on medium speed until light and fluffy. Add eggs, one at a time, beating until smooth. Spoon warm batter into a pastry bag fitted with a ½-inch star tip.

Pour oil into a large skillet to a depth of 2 inches. Heat oil to 370°. Squeeze juice from lime (save lime juice for another use). Add lime shell to oil (lime will flavor churros as they cook). Pipe batter onto oil in 4- to 5-inch lengths (do not crowd churros). Cook until golden brown, turning occasionally, about 1½ to 2 minutes. Remove churros from oil using a slotted spoon. Drain on a wire rack set over paper towels. Repeat procedure with remaining butter.

Combine ¼ cup sugar and cinnamon in a shallow dish; roll warm churros in mixture. Serve warm.

Note: Churros can be prepared 6 hours ahead. Before serving, place on a cookie sheet and reheat in a 250° oven for 5 minutes.

Caramelized Flan with Cinnamon Sugar Tortillas

Serves 6.

Caramel
¾ cup granulated sugar
Custard
2 cups half and half
⅓ cup granulated sugar
8 egg yolks, at room temperature, beaten
¼ cup dark rum
2 teaspoons vanilla
Tortillas
1 tablespoon granulated sugar
1½ teaspoons ground cinnamon
Vegetable oil for deep-fat frying
6 4-inch flour tortillas *

For caramel, heat a medium heavy skillet over medium-low heat for 2 minutes. Gradually add ¾ cup sugar, stirring constantly until dissolved. Heat until sugar turns a rich golden brown; swirling skillet occasionally and watching carefully to prevent burning, about 20 minutes. Do not stir. Remove from heat. Immediately spoon caramel into six 8-ounce ramekins or custard cups, turning so caramel coats bottoms and sides; set aside.

Preheat oven to 350°. For custard, combine half and half and ⅓ cup sugar in a heavy, 2-quart saucepan over medium-low heat, stirring until sugar dissolves; simmer. Beat together egg yolks, rum, and vanilla in a large bowl. Whisk in 1 cup hot half and half mixture. Gradually whisk egg yolk mixture into remaining hot half and half mixture; stir for 1 minute. Remove from heat. Pour custard into caramelized ramekins. Place ramekins in a shallow roasting pan. Pour in enough simmering water to come halfway up sides of cups. Bake for 25 minutes or until a knife inserted in center comes out clean. Remove ramekins from water. Cool on a wire rack to room temperature. Refrigerate until well chilled, about 3 hours.

Continued on next page

For tortillas, stir together 1 tablespoon sugar and cinnamon in a cup; set aside. Cut tortilla rounds into sixths. Pour oil into a large skillet to a depth of ½-inch. Heat oil over medium-high heat until 370°. Fry tortilla pieces in hot oil in batches, turning once until golden brown, about 50 seconds. Drain tortillas on paper towels. Repeat with remaining tortillas. Sprinkle cinnamon-sugar mixture over warm tortillas.

To serve, invert ramekins onto serving platter. If necessary tap cups to release. (If caramel sticks, cover bottom of cups with a hot towel until caramel melts; spoon over flan.) Serve with cinnamon-sugar tortillas.

Note: Flan and tortillas can be made 1 day in advance.

Fruit Gazpacho with Citrus Dressing

Simple and straightforward, this fresh and colorful salad can be served for brunch or dessert. Feel free to substitute any variety of fruit. Depending upon the sweetness of the fruit you use, it may be necessary to adjust the amount of sugar in the dressing.
Serves 8.

3 bananas, peeled and diced
2 mangoes, peeled and diced
1 pineapple, peeled, cored, and diced
2 cups seedless grapes, quartered
Citrus Dressing
2 tablespoons fresh orange juice
2 teaspoons fresh lime juice
2 teaspoons granulated sugar
¼ teaspoon ground cardamom

Combine bananas, mangoes, pineapple, and grapes in a serving bowl; set aside.

For dressing, combine orange juice, lime juice, sugar, and cardamom in a small bowl; blend until sugar is dissolved. Pour dressing over fruit; toss gently.

Café Mexicano

Piloncillo is an intensely sweet flavoring used in south of the border cookery. It can be purchased at Latin American specialty stores. If unavailable, for this recipe substitute 3 tablespoons dark brown sugar.
Serves 8.

2 tablespoons Mexican piloncillo or 3 tablespoons dark
   brown sugar
2 2-inch sticks cinnamon
½ ounce semi-sweet chocolate, grated
8 cups hot strong coffee
Kahlua (optional)
Cinnamon sticks (optional)
Whipped cream (optional)

Combine piloncillo or brown sugar, cinnamon sticks, and chocolate in a heavy, 3-quart saucepan. Pour in hot coffee. Place saucepan over low heat, stirring until piloncillo and chocolate dissolve. Let steep for at least 15 minutes or up to 1 hour before serving. Pour into mugs. Pass Kahlua, cinnamon sticks, and whipped cream separately, if desired.

A Bridesmaids' Tea

Phyllo-Wrapped Brie Stuffed with Ham and Cheese
Currant Cream Scones
Victorian Tea Sponges Filled with Berries and Cream
Chesire Cheese Scones
Lemon Curd
Devonshire Cream
Marmalade and Assorted Preserves
Tea

love the British custom of afternoon tea—it is a wonderfully civilized way to fill the gap between lunch and dinner. The art of entertaining at tea time is one of the most popular classes I teach. More and more of America's best restaurants and hotels are introducing high teas instead of traditional happy hours.

Menu planning for a tea party is easy, and everything should be made in advance. Prepare an assortment of dainty sweet and savory foods to be accompanied by a pot of piping hot tea. English-style tea is served straight or with milk. "Tea first or milk first?" is the utterly proper question to pose before pouring since staunch Anglophiles insist they can tell the difference.

An intimate setting including a table set with fine china, linens or lace, and a bouquet of fresh flowers perfects a traditional tea fit for a gathering of special friends.

Currant Cream Scones, Chesire Cheese Scones, Lemon Curd, Devonshire Cream, and Victorian Tea Sponges Filled with Berries and Cream

Phyllo-Wrapped Brie Filled with Ham and Cheese

Simple, elegant, and delicious. The wheel is baked just long enough to soften the Brie and brown the phyllo leaves. *Serves 8.*

    1 8-ounce wheel Brie cheese
    2 ounces smoked or peppered ham, thinly sliced
    2 ounces Swiss cheese, thinly sliced
    2 to 4 tablespoons minced parsley or spinach
    6 sheets frozen phyllo dough, thawed
    6 tablespoons unsalted clarified butter, melted *

Grease a 15½ × 10½ × 1-inch jelly roll pan; set aside. Preheat oven to 350°. Split Brie in half horizontally. Evenly lay sliced ham over one half of Brie. Top with Swiss cheese and sprinkle with parsley. Place remaining Brie half on top; press firmly making sure there are no cracks.

Place a slightly damp cloth on the counter. Place 3 phyllo leaves on cloth; brush with melted butter. Place Brie in center of phyllo; wrap phyllo around Brie. Place remaining phyllo on a damp cloth; brush with butter. Place wrapped Brie, folded side down, in center of phyllo dough; wrap phyllo around Brie. Place wrapped Brie, folded side down, on prepared jelly roll pan. Brush top with remaining melted butter. Bake for 25 to 35 minutes or until golden brown. Let stand for 10 to 15 minutes. Serve warm.

Currant Cream Scones

These rich biscuits are wonderful for a mid-morning coffee break. Warm from the oven, they are a year-round favorite. *Makes 2 dozen.*

    3¼ cups all-purpose flour
    ½ cup granulated sugar
    4 teaspoons cream of tartar
    2 teaspoons baking soda
    1 teaspoon salt
    6 tablespoons unsalted butter, well-chilled
    1 cup dried currants or raisins
    1½ to 2 cups whipping cream
    1 egg, lightly beaten

Preheat oven to 400°. Combine flour, sugar, cream of tartar, baking soda, and salt in a large bowl. Cut in butter using a pastry blender or two knives used scissor-fashion until mixture resembles coarse crumbs. Stir in currants or raisins. Mix in 1 cup whipping cream. Add enough additional whipping cream to form a soft—but not sticky—dough. Turn dough out onto a lightly floured surface and knead gently until dough holds together, about 30 seconds. Divide dough in half. Gently pat dough into a 6- to 8-inch circle, about ½-inch thick. Cut each circle into 12 wedges. Arrange wedges on baking sheets. Brush tops with beaten egg. Bake for 10 minutes or until golden. Serve warm.

Variation: For Lemon Cream Scones, omit currants and add 3 tablespoons finely grated lemon peel. Bake as directed.

Victorian Tea Sponges Filled with Berries and Cream

Serves 8.

Cake
½ cup ground skinned hazelnuts
½ cup ground blanched almonds
½ cup confectioners' sugar
½ cup cake flour, sifted
¼ cup granulated sugar
3 egg yolks, at room temperature
3 egg whites, at room temperature

Filling
1 cup whipping cream
1½ cups fresh raspberries, rinsed
½ cup confectioners' sugar

Line baking sheets with parchment paper or waxed paper. Grease paper lightly. Draw eight 4-inch circles on paper. Fit a pastry bag with a ½-inch (#6) round pastry tip. Sprinkle two clean dish towels with confectioners' sugar. Position oven rack in lower third of oven. Preheat oven to 350°.

For cake, combine hazelnuts and almonds in a small mixing bowl. Sift ½ cup confectioners' sugar over nuts; stir to blend. Remove 3 tablespoons nut mixture; reserve. Add flour to remaining nut mixture; stir to blend. Beat egg yolks and reserved 3 tablespoons of nut mixture in a 1½ quart mixing bowl on high speed until light and pale, about 2 to 3 minutes. Set aside. Whip egg whites in a clean mixing bowl with clean beaters on medium-low speed until frothy, about 30 seconds. Increase speed to medium and gradually add granulated sugar, beating until soft peaks form. Increase speed to high; beat until glossy white and stiff, about 1½ to 2 minutes. Gently pour egg yolk mixture over whites; fold mixtures together using a rubber spatula. Sprinkle half of nut mixture over egg mixture; gently fold. Repeat procedure with remaining nut mixture. Gently spoon batter into prepared pastry bag. Pipe a 1-inch line lengthwise, beginning in center of the circle. Use this line as a guide, spiraling the batter around it. Apply just enough pressure to the pastry bag so that the amount forced out is no larger than the ½-inch diameter of the pastry tip. Bake for 8 to 10 minutes or until light brown at the edges and springy but firm to touch. Do not overcook. Invert sponge rounds onto prepared towels. Gently peel paper lining off. If paper begins to stick, sprinkle cold water over paper. Fold sponges carefully in half (they may crack). Cool sponges on towel.

For filling, beat whipping cream in a chilled bowl with chilled beaters until stiff. Gently fill a pastry bag fitted with a fluted tip. Pipe whipped cream into each sponge until full. Decoratively place raspberries on whipped cream. Dust with remaining ½ cup confectioners' sugar.

Chesire Cheese Scones

Take care not to overbake scones or they will become dry and hard.
Makes 1 dozen.

  2 cups all-purpose flour
  2½ teaspoons baking powder
  1 teaspoon salt
  Pinch of cayenne pepper
  2 tablespoons unsalted butter, well-chilled
  1 cup plus 2 tablespoons grated Chesire or cheddar cheese
  1 egg
  ⅔ to ¾ cup milk
Glaze
  1 egg
  1 teaspoon water
  2 tablespoons freshly grated Parmesan cheese

Preheat oven to 400°. Sift together flour, baking powder, salt, and cayenne pepper in a large bowl. Cut in butter using a pastry blender or two knives used scissor-fashion until mixture resembles coarse crumbs. Stir in Chesire or cheddar cheese. Beat together 1 egg and ⅔ cup milk. Add egg mixture to flour mixture. Stir mixture, adding more milk if necessary, until dough is sticky but manageable. Knead dough gently on a lightly floured surface for 30 seconds. Gently roll dough out to ¾-inch thickness, lightly flouring as necessary to prevent sticking. Cut out dough using a floured 2-inch round cutter (push straight down, do not twist). Arrange scones on baking sheets.

For glaze, combine 1 egg and water. Brush tops of scones with egg mixture. Sprinkle Parmesan cheese over scones. Bake for 10 to 12 minutes or until golden brown and crusty. Serve warm or at room temperature.

Lemon Curd

You can substitute lime juice, orange juice, and grapefruit juice for the lemon juice. Lemon curd is delicious spread on toast, crumpets, and scones, or spooned into individual pre-baked tart shells.
Makes 2 cups.

  1⅓ cups granulated sugar
  ¾ cup plus 2 tablespoons unsalted butter, softened
  ⅔ cup fresh lemon juice, strained
  4 eggs, at room temperature
  4 egg yolks, at room temperature
  1 tablespoon finely grated lemon peel

Combine sugar, butter, lemon juice, eggs, egg yolks, and lemon peel in top of a non-aluminum double boiler set over boiling water. Whisk mixture continuously until thick enough to coat the back of a metal spoon. Do not boil. Transfer mixture to a non-aluminum bowl. Cool to room temperature. Store in tightly sealed containers. Refrigerate until ready to serve. Store in the refrigerator for up to 3 months.

Devonshire Cream

The specialty of Devonshire, England, is a clotted cream. The traditional English cream tea consists of clotted cream and preserves spread on scones. This recipe is an easy make-at-home version that can be prepared several days in advance. *Makes 2 cups.*

    2 cups sour cream
    2 tablespoons confectioners' sugar, sifted
    1 teaspoon vanilla

    Stir together sour cream, sugar, and vanilla in a bowl. Cover and refrigerate until ready to use.

5
Breezy Summer Parties

A Father's Day Brunch
A Mad Hatter's Tea
Cool Down Dessert Party
Poolside Refresher
A Sensational Baby Shower
A Summer Soirée

A Father's Day Brunch

Chilled Strawberry-Rhubarb Soup
Cheese Blintzes with Blueberry Compote
Upside-Down Cinnamon Donut Apple Pudding
Peach and Prosciutto Salad with Mango Dressing
Sparkling Raspberry Kir

Celebrate June, the beginning of summer, by honoring dad with this spectacular brunch. This menu takes full advantage of fresh produce at its peak, flaunting flavors and colors which work together to create dishes that are bound to be memorable. Summer fruits are used to reinterpret even the classic soup and salad combination: Chilled Strawberry-Rhubarb Soup and a Peach and Prosciutto Salad with Mango Dressing. The menu is rounded out with Cheese Blintzes with Blueberry Compote and Upside-Down Cinnamon Donut Apple Pudding, which are bound to become year-round family favorites—not just reserved for this special occasion.

The best table linens and serving pieces for this occasion are in masculine colors—navy, burgundy, forest green, brown. The ubiquitous Father's Day tie is a lively alternative to a traditional centerpiece.

Peach and Prosciutto Salad with Mango Dressing, Sparkling Raspberry Kir, and Chilled Strawberry-Rhubarb Soup

Chilled Strawberry-Rhubarb Soup

Enhanced by the slightly tangy flavor of crème fraîche and the sweetness of fresh strawberries, this delectable soup is a sophisticated starter for brunch or dinner.
Serves 4 to 6.

1 pound rhubarb, sliced into 1-inch pieces
1 pint strawberries, rinsed and hulled
3 cups fresh orange juice
2 to 3 tablespoons granulated sugar
1 tablespoon finely grated lemon peel
1½ tablespoons cornstarch
1 cup plus 2 tablespoons champagne
½ cup whipping cream
½ cup Crème Fraîche (For recipe, see page 140.)
Crème Fraîche
Mint leaves
Sliced strawberries

Combine rhubarb, strawberries, and orange juice in a medium saucepan over medium-high heat. Bring to a boil. Reduce heat to low and simmer for 20 minutes, stirring occasionally. Remove from heat. Purée mixture in a blender or food processor; press through a fine sieve. Return mixture to saucepan. Stir in sugar and lemon peel. Bring mixture to a simmer.

Mix cornstarch with ⅓ cup champagne. Pour into fruit mixture and simmer for 5 minutes, stirring occasionally. Remove from heat. Combine whipping cream and Crème Fraîche in a small bowl. Stir cream mixture into soup. Stir in remaining champagne. Transfer mixture to a serving bowl. Cover and refrigerate for at least 4 hours or overnight. Garnish with Crème Fraîche, mint, and strawberries.

Cheese Blintzes with Blueberry Compote

This lovely old-fashioned brunch favorite has been updated for contemporary tastes.
Makes 16 to 20 blintzes.

Basic Dessert Crêpe
For recipe, see page 142.
Filling
3 8-ounce containers ricotta cheese
3 eggs
¼ cup granulated sugar
1 tablespoon vanilla
1 teaspoon finely grated lemon peel
Pinch of salt
Blueberry Compote
4 teaspoons cornstarch
2 tablespoons water
2 cups fresh blueberries, rinsed
½ cup granulated sugar
½ cup Grand Marnier
9 tablespoons unsalted butter

Prepare Basic Dessert Crêpes as directed.

For filling, combine ricotta cheese, eggs, ¼ cup sugar, vanilla, lemon peel, and salt in a medium bowl, stirring until smooth. Cover and refrigerate for 1 hour.

Meanwhile, prepare Blueberry Compote. Mix cornstarch and water in a cup until smooth. Combine blueberries and ½ cup sugar in a medium saucepan, lightly crushing about one quarter of the berries with a spoon. Add cornstarch mixture and Grand Marnier. Cook over medium heat, stirring frequently, until thickened, about 3 to 5 minutes. Remove from heat.

To assemble, place about 2 tablespoons cheese mixture in center of each crêpe, cooked side up. Fold in opposite edges towards center until edges meet. Then fold in remaining edges making a rectangular envelope. Repeat procedure with remaining crêpes and filling.

Melt 3 tablespoons of the butter in a 12-inch skillet over medium-high heat. Place blintzes in pan, seam side down. Fry carefully, turning once, until golden brown. Melt remaining butter and fry remaining blintzes.

Place blintzes on individual plates or a serving tray. Top with warm Blueberry Compote. (If compote becomes too thick, thin with a little water and gently reheat.)

Upside-Down Cinnamon Donut Apple Pudding

The proof is in the pudding of this version of a recipe author Linda Zimmerman developed as a new take on the classic apple tarte tatin. The secret to perfect carmelization is to use a heavy gauge cake pan or a cast iron skillet on medium-low heat.
Serves 6 to 8.

8 day-old cinnamon cake donuts, broken into bits
1 cup milk
¼ cup whipping cream
3 eggs, lightly beaten
1 teaspoon vanilla
½ cup unsalted butter
¾ cup granulated sugar
8 or 9 small (about 2¼ pounds) Red Delicious apples
1 cup dried currants or raisins
Sweetened Whipped Cream
For recipe, see page 141.

Place broken donuts in a large mixing bowl. Beat together milk, whipping cream, eggs, and vanilla in a separate bowl. Pour milk mixture over donuts; set aside.

Spead 6 tablespoons of the butter over the surface of a heavy 9-inch cast iron skillet or heavy gauge cake pan. Sprinkle ½ cup granulated sugar over pan; set aside.

Slice off the tops and bottoms of the apples so they have flat ends. Peel, core, and quarter apples. Arrange apple on their sides, setting on cut end and facing the same direction in the pan. Sprinkle currants or raisins and remaining sugar over apples. Dot remaining butter over apples. (If all the apples don't fit in a single layer, then layer the extra apples on top of each other.)

Cook apples over medium-low heat for 20 to 25 minutes or until apples begin to soften. Push remaining apples down into the pan towards the center until all the apples fit in the pan. Cook for 35 to 40 minutes more or until apple syrup has caramelized and is bubbly and dark golden brown. Be careful not to allow the caramel to burn.

Remove from heat. Pour donut mixture over apples. Preheat oven to 350°. Place skillet or cake pan in a roasting pan. Pour in boiling water until it reaches halfway up the sides of the skillet. Bake for 45 to 50 minutes or until pudding is puffy and golden. Cool in pan for 5 minutes. Run a knife around the edge of the pudding; invert onto a serving platter.

Prepare Sweetened Whipped Cream as directed. Serve with pudding.

Variation: Replace apples with an equal amount of pears and add 1 teaspoon ground ginger to batter.

Peach and Prosciutto Salad with Mango Dressing

Sue Young and Cathy Thomas, owners of The Tasting Spoon in Los Angeles, feature this salad in their summer entertaining classes.
Serves 8.

4 peaches, peeled, halved, pitted, and sliced
2 tablespoons fresh lemon juice
4 ounces prosciutto, finely shredded
4 ounces Gorgonzola cheese, crumbled
4 tablespoons chopped pistachio nuts
Dressing
2 mangoes, peeled, pitted, and coarsely chopped
4 tablespoons peach schnapps
2 teaspoons rice wine vinegar
Assorted tender greens (i.e., baby lettuce, watercress, and arugula) rinsed and dried
8 large mint leaves

Combine peaches and lemon juice in a bowl. Add prosciutto, cheese, and nuts; set aside.

For dressing, purée mangoes in a blender or food processor. Add schnapps and vinegar; blend well. Toss dressing with peach mixture. Arrange greens on salad plates. Evenly divide peach mixture over greens. Garnish with mint.

Sparkling Raspberry Kir

Serves 8.

8 fresh raspberries, rinsed
24 tablespoons raspberry liqueur
1 750-milliliter bottle brut champagne

Place 1 raspberry in the bottom of 8 champagne flutes. Pour 3 tablespoons liqueur over each raspberry. Pour champagne over liqueur until glasses are full.

A Mad Hatter's Tea

English Summer Pudding
Miniature Almond Macaroons
Date Nut Pinwheels
Champagne Grape Tartlets
Strawberry and Kiwi Shortbreads

A Mad Hatter's Tea party can help make summer what people want it to be—fun, easy, and festive. Just as Alice found when she sat down with the March Hare, the Hatter, and the Dormouse for tea, the menu here features old-fashioned desserts with some innovative twists: Date Nut Pinwheels are not only visually appealing, but a delicious do-ahead cookie; grape tartlets have been scaled down with the use of champagne grapes; and shortbread wedges replace traditional shortcakes in individual Strawberry and Kiwi Shortbreads.

Create a whimsical mood with offbeat colors, textures, patterns, shapes, and styles. Bring the creations of artists to the table with their new versions of tableware. At A Mad Hatter's Tea party anything goes, so be bold and creative in choosing serving pieces—and don't forget the "eat me" and "drink me" place cards.

English Summer Pudding

The secret to this pudding is to have enough juice and berries so that the bread layers absorb the fresh fruit flavors and colors. If fresh currants are available, use them in place of 1½ cups of fresh berries.
Serves 8.

1½ cups fresh strawberries, rinsed, hulled, and quartered
1½ cups fresh blueberries, rinsed
1½ cups fresh raspberries, rinsed
1½ cups fresh blackberries, rinsed
⅓ cup granulated sugar
¼ cup Grand Marnier
2 teaspoons finely grated lemon peel
1 loaf unsliced homemade-style white bread
Lime Crème Fraîche
For recipe, see page 140.
Fresh raspberries

Toss together strawberries, blueberries, raspberries, and blackberries in a medium saucepan. Stir in sugar, Grand Marnier, and lemon peel. Cook over medium heat, stirring until sugar dissolves. Do not overcook. Set aside.

Using a serrated knife, trim the crust off the bread. Cut the bread into ½-inch slices. Cut each slice diagonally to form triangles. Line the bottom and sides of a 1½- to 2-quart non-corrosive bowl with some of the bread slices. Cut bread into small pieces to fit any gaps so the bowl is completely lined.

Spoon one half of berry mixture into bread-lined bowl. Top with a layer of bread slices to completely cover fruit. Spoon remaining berry mixture over bread. Top completely with remaining bread slices.

Place a plate slightly smaller than the bowl on top of the bread and berry mixture. Weigh down with a 1-pound weight or can. Refrigerate at least 8 hours or overnight. Carefully unmold by inverting pudding onto a serving plate. Serve with Lime Crème Fraîche. Garnish with fresh raspberries.

Miniature Almond Macaroons

Flaked coconut instead of shredded coconut improves the texture of these cookies.
Makes 2½ dozen.

2⅔ cups flaked coconut
⅔ cup granulated sugar
½ cup all-purpose flour
¼ teaspoon salt
4 egg whites, at room temperature
1 teaspoon almond extract
1 cup finely chopped blanched almonds

Line 2 baking sheets with aluminum foil. Preheat oven to 325°. Combine coconut, sugar, flour, and salt in a medium bowl; set aside. Beat egg whites in a medium mixing bowl on medium-high speed until foamy. Add almond extract; beat until stiff. Fold in coconut mixture. Fold in almonds. Drop from teaspoonfuls onto prepared baking sheets. Bake for 20 to 25 minutes or until edges are golden brown. Remove from baking sheets. Cool on wire racks.

Strawberry and Kiwi Shortbreads, Champagne Grape Tartlets, Miniature Almond Macaroons, and Date Nut Pinwheels

Date Nut Pinwheels

Date Nut Pinwheels are delicious warm from the oven served with a glass of iced cold milk. Freeze the unbaked cookie roll, then slice and bake the cookies as needed.
Makes about 4½ dozen.

1 pound pitted dates, finely chopped
½ cup water
½ cup granulated sugar
1 cup chopped walnuts or pecans
½ cup butter
½ cup light brown sugar
½ cup granulated sugar
1 egg
½ teaspoon vanilla
1¾ cups all-purpose flour
½ teaspoon baking soda
½ teaspoon salt

Combine dates, water, and ½ cup granulated sugar in a saucepan over medium-high heat, stirring constantly until thickened, about 5 minutes. Stir in nuts. Cool.

Preheat oven to 400°. Beat butter, brown sugar, and ½ cup granulated sugar in a medium mixing bowl. Stir in egg. Add vanilla. Beat in flour, baking soda, and salt. Form dough into a ball; wrap in plastic wrap and refrigerate for 30 minutes.

Roll dough out onto a lightly floured surface to a 12 × 14-inch rectangle. Spread date filling evenly over dough leaving a 1-inch border. Roll dough jelly-roll fashion, starting with long side. Wrap roll in plastic wrap. Chill for 30 minutes. Slice dough into ¼-inch slices. Place on a baking sheet. Bake for 8 to 10 minutes.

Champagne Grape Tartlets

Serves 8.

Crust
1½ cups all-purpose flour
¼ cup finely ground blanched almonds
3 tablespoons firmly packed light brown sugar
Pinch of salt
½ cup unsalted butter, chilled and cut into pieces
1 egg, lightly beaten
1 teaspoon finely grated lemon peel
½ teaspoon vanilla

Filling
¾ pound champagne grapes or green or purple seedless grapes, rinsed
¾ cup apricot preserves
3 tablespoon dry sherry
Confectioners' sugar

For crust, combine flour, almonds, brown sugar, and salt in a bowl. Cut in butter until mixture resembles coarse crumbs. Combine egg, lemon peel, and vanilla in a cup. Add to flour mixture; stir until moist and dough holds together when formed into a ball. Wrap in plastic wrap. Refrigerate for 30 minutes.

Butter eight 3- to 3½-inch tartlet pans (preferably with removable bottoms). Divide dough into 8 equal pieces. Press each piece into prepared tartlet pans. Chill tartlets for 30 minutes.

Preheat oven to 400°. Line tartlet shells with a square of foil, and fill with uncooked rice or dried beans. Bake on a baking sheet for 10 minutes. Reduce oven temperature to 350°. Bake for 15 to 20 minutes or until golden brown. Cool in pans for 10 minutes. Remove foil and rice or beans. Carefully remove tartlet shells from pans and cool on wire racks; cool completely.

Combine preserves and sherry in a small pan over medium-low heat, stirring until melted. Press mixture through a fine sieve. Brush preserve mixture on bottoms of cooled tartlet shells. Arrange grapes in a decorative pattern over preserve mixture. Brush remaining preserve mixture over grapes and edges of tartlets. (Reheat, if necessary.) Dust lightly with confectioners' sugar. Serve at room temperature.

Strawberry and Kiwi Shortbreads

For a very quick and easy, last-minute summer dessert, substitute purchased Petticoat Tails shortbread. It can be found in better supermarkets or gourmet food stores.
Serves 8.

Shortbread
    1½ cups unsalted butter
    ¾ cup granulated sugar
    3 cups all-purpose flour
    1½ cups rice flour (available in the Asian section of many
        grocery stores or at most health food stores)

Filling
    1 cup whipping cream
    1 3-ounce package cream cheese, softened
    ½ cup confectioners' sugar
    1 tablespoon finely grated orange peel
    1 tablespoon Grand Marnier
    4 kiwi fruit, peeled and sliced
    4 cups (about 1½ pounds) sliced fresh strawberries
    2 tablespoons granulated sugar
    8 jumbo strawberries, rinsed, with the stems on

For shortbread, preheat oven to 350°. Beat butter in a medium mixing bowl on medium speed until smooth. Gradually add ¾ cup granulated sugar; beat until light and fluffy. Sift flour and rice flour into a bowl. Add flour mixture, one third at a time, to butter mixture, beating well. Divide dough equally between three 9-inch pie plates. Press dough evenly into each pan. Smooth edges with fingers. Score shortbread into 8 wedges with a sharp knife. With the tines of a fork, prick dough about every ½ inch. (Use a decorative shortbread press, if desired.) Bake for 25 to 30 minutes or until light brown. Cool in pan for 5 minutes. Invert shortbreads onto a wire rack. Cool completely. Gently break shortbreads into wedges. Store in an airtight container until ready to serve.

For filling, beat whipping cream in a chilled bowl with chilled beaters until soft. Beat in cream cheese. Gradually add confectioners' sugar. Stir in orange peel and Grand Marnier. Cover and refrigerate until ready to serve.

Toss sliced kiwi fruit and strawberries together in a bowl. Sprinkle 2 tablespoons granulated sugar over fruit; gently toss.

To assemble, arrange 3 shortbread wedges on individual serving plates. Place a dollop of whipped cream mixture over shortbreads. Place about ½ cup fruit mixture on top. Garnish each serving with a whole strawberry.

Cool Down Dessert Party

Hazelnut Polenta Ice Cream Sandwiches
Frozen Macaroon Dessert
Vanilla Bean Ice Cream
Chocolate-Orange Sorbet
Ice Cream Cones
Raspberry-Blueberry Sauce
Mocha Sauce

t is hard to imagine summer without ice cream, that cool frozen confection that captures the flavor of the season and tantalizes the taste buds as it slowly melts on the tongue. For the ultimate summer party, consider a gathering of friends where the focus is on cool and refreshing desserts. An ice cream social can take on many forms—maybe a buffet of selected frozen desserts with an adjacent sundae bar where guests can come up with their own concoctions. The recipes presented here were created for adults, but children will definitely find some favorites.

Vanilla Bean Ice Cream Cones with Raspberry-Blueberry Sauce and Mocha Sauce

Hazelnut Polenta Ice Cream Sandwiches

Hazelnut Polenta cookies, which have a texture similar to peanut butter cookies, are made into ice cream sandwiches topped with melted chocolate. This is definitely not kid's stuff.
Makes about 6 sandwiches.

¾ cup unsalted butter
½ cup granulated sugar
¼ cup firmly packed light brown sugar
1 egg yolk
1 teaspoon vanilla
1 cup all-purpose flour
½ cup fine polenta or yellow cornmeal
1 teaspoon baking powder
½ teaspoon ground nutmeg
½ teaspoon ground cloves
⅔ cup finely chopped, skinned hazelnuts, toasted
1 pint desired ice cream, softened
3 ounces semi-sweet chocolate, chopped

Line baking sheets with parchment paper; set aside. Preheat oven to 350°. Beat butter and sugars until light and fluffy in a medium mixing bowl. Beat in egg yolk and vanilla. Stir together flour, polenta, baking powder, nutmeg, and cloves. Add to butter mixture, beating till well combined. Stir in hazelnuts.

Roll dough about ¼-inch thick between two pieces of waxed paper. Cut dough using a 2½-inch round cookie cutter. Place cookie rounds 3 inches apart on prepared baking sheets. Bake for 10 to 12 minutes or until golden brown. Cool for 5 minutes, then transfer to wire racks. Cool completely.

To assemble one ice cream sandwich at a time, place 1 cookie, flat side up, on a work surface. Scoop about ¼ cup ice cream on cookie. Top with a second cookie, flat side down. Press cookies together to flatten ice cream. Repeat procedure with remaining cookies and ice cream. Wrap each ice cream sandwich in plastic wrap and freeze until firm, about 4 hours or overnight.

Melt chocolate in top of a double boiler over simmering water stirring until smooth. Dip a fork into chocolate and drizzle free-form lines over tops of sandwiches. Freeze until chocolate is firm.

Note: Hazelnut Polenta Ice Cream Sandwiches can be prepared 3 to 5 days in advance.

Frozen Macaroon Dessert

This recipe dates back to the Officer's Wives Club during the early '60s. This easy sherbet dessert was a family summertime treat.
Serves 8.

2 cups whipping cream
2 tablespoons confectioners' sugar
1 teaspoon vanilla
18 crispy macaroon cookies, crumbled
1 cup chopped pecans
1 quart rainbow sherbet or sorbet (or 1 pint each of two complementing flavors), softened
½ cup chopped pecans (optional)

Beat whipping cream in a chilled bowl with chilled beaters until stiff. Beat in confectioners' sugar and vanilla. Fold in macaroons and 1 cup pecans. Put half of macaroon mixture in a 9 × 13-inch baking pan. Spread softened sherbet or sorbet over macaroon mixture. Cut a knife through sherbet to marble. Spread remaining macaroon mixture over sherbet. Sprinkle additional ½ cup chopped nuts over mixture, if desired. Cover with aluminum foil. Freeze until solid, about 4 to 6 hours. To unmold. Place pan in a hot water bath for 1 minute. Run a knife along sides to loosen.

Note: To create a bombe, spread half of macaroon mixture along the bottom and sides of a metal mixing bowl. Layer alternating colors of sherbet inside bowl. Top with an even layer of remaining macaroon mixture. Freeze.

Vanilla Bean Ice Cream

Makes about 1 quart.

2 cups whipping cream
1¼ cups milk
2 vanilla beans, split
10 egg yolks
¾ cup granulated sugar

Combine 1¼ cups of the whipping cream, milk, and vanilla beans in a medium, heavy saucepan over medium heat. Bring mixture just to boiling. Reduce heat to low.

Whisk egg yolks in a large mixing bowl until light. Gradually whisk in sugar till well combined. Gradually whisk hot cream mixture into egg yolk mixture. Return to saucepan and cook over medium heat, stirring constantly, until mixture thickens and coats the back of a metal spoon, about 3 minutes. Do not overcook or eggs may curdle. Pour into a clean bowl. Cover and let cool to room temperature.

Remove vanilla beans and scrape seeds into custard. Discard pods. Stir in remaining ¾ cup whipping cream. Strain mixture through a fine sieve. Pour into an ice cream canister. Process according to manufacturer's directions.

Chocolate-Orange Sorbet

Unlike sherbet, sorbet never contains milk. This recipe is best made with Dutch-process cocoa powder, which has been treated with an alkali to help neutralize the cocoa's natural acidity, making it less bitter tasting.
Makes about 1 quart.

1½ cups water
¼ cup unsweetened cocoa powder, preferably Dutch process
2 tablespoons granulated sugar
2 tablespoons light corn syrup
6 ounces bittersweet chocolate, chopped
¼ cup fresh orange juice
1 tablespoon finely grated orange peel
¾ cup water

Combine 1½ cups water, cocoa powder, sugar, and corn syrup in a medium, heavy saucepan over medium heat. Bring mixture to a boil, stirring constantly until mixture is smooth. Reduce heat to low. Add chocolate, stirring until smooth. Stir in orange juice, orange peel, and ¾ cup water. Remove from heat.

Pour mixture into an ice cream canister. Process according to manufacturer's directions. Transfer sorbet to a covered container and freeze overnight to allow flavors to mellow.

Ice Cream Cones

Homemade ice cream cones filled with your favorite ice cream are sure to be a hit. Waffle cones can be made with a "pizzelle" maker, an Italian appliance found in gourmet and specialty stores. There are two basic types of pizzelle makers; one resembles a manual tortilla press and the other is electric. Be sure to follow the manufacturer's directions for cooking. *Makes 8 cones.*

2 eggs, at room temperature
¾ cup confectioners' sugar, sifted
½ cup plus 2 tablespoons all-purpose flour
½ teaspoon vanilla
Pinch of salt
2 tablespoons finely chopped nuts (hazelnuts, macademia nuts, pecans, or pistachios)
8 ounces semi-sweet chocolate, chopped
Assorted toppings (chopped nuts, candy sprinkles, shredded coconut) (optional)
Desired ice cream

Preheat oven to 425°. Lightly butter and flour two baking sheets. Trace a 6-inch round pattern onto floured baking sheets; set aside.

Whisk together eggs and sugar in a medium bowl until smooth. Stir in flour, vanilla, and salt until smooth. Spoon 2 tablespoons batter into center of one of the circles. Using a narrow spatula, spread batter to completely coat the circle. Repeat with remaining batter. Sprinkle each circle with nuts. Bake for 4 to 6 minutes or until light golden at edges of circles. Do not overcook. Run a thin-bladed knife or spatula under one of the cookies. Working quickly, roll the cookie into a cone so that the side that was against the baking sheet is the outside of the cones. Place the cones upright in small glasses to cool. Repeat with remaining cookies. If cookies become too firm to shape, place them back in the oven for 1 to 2 minutes to soften.

Melt chocolate in top of a double boiler set over simmering water, stirring until smooth. Remove from heat. Dip wide end of cones into melted chocolate. Before chocolate dries, dip cone into assorted toppings, if desired. Allow chocolate to set before filling with ice cream.

Raspberry-Blueberry Sauce

Makes about 1 cup.

⅓ cup water
¼ cup granulated sugar
1 cup fresh blueberries, rinsed
1 cup fresh raspberries, rinsed
1 teaspoon fresh lemon juice
½ cup fresh raspberries, rinsed and cut into quarters

Combine water and sugar in a small saucepan over medium-high heat. Bring mixture to a boil, stirring constantly until sugar dissolves. Cool syrup to room temperature.

Meanwhile, purée blueberries and raspberries in a blender or food processor. Strain berries through a fine sieve into a medium bowl; discard seeds. Stir syrup and lemon juice into berry puree. Fold in cut raspberries. Cover and refrigerate for at least two hours or overnight.

Mocha Sauce

Makes about 2 cups.

½ cup water
½ cup unsalted butter, cut into pieces
6 tablespoons light corn syrup
2 tablespoons brandy
1 teaspoon instant coffee crystals
Pinch of salt
8 ounces semi-sweet chocolate, chopped

Combine water, butter, corn syrup, brandy, coffee crystals, and salt in a medium saucepan over medium-high heat. Bring mixture to a boil, stirring occasionally. Remove from heat. Add chocolate; stir until smooth. Serve hot or at room temperature.

Poolside Refresher

Watermelon with Blackberries
Roasted Peach Tart
Mile-High Strawberry Pie with
Chocolate-Orange Cookie Crust
Citrus-Scented Poppy Seed Cake
Grilled Fruit Kabobs
Lemon-Lime Summer Coolers

Grilling and summertime are a synonymous part of American life. Transform a hot humid evening into a balmy night in the tropics with a poolside dessert party, a grand finale to a traditional barbecue of burgers and hot dogs. This collection of light, colorful, and easy-to-prepare desserts make the most of summer fruits at their peak of ripeness and abundance.

Begin by covering your table with an elaborately decorated tablecloth. Then add a brilliant accent with colorful handblown glassware. Capture the mood of the tropics by illuminating the table with candlelight or with luminarias set around the pool.

Watermelon with Blackberries

A splash of sparkling wine and fresh blackberries dress up a summer fruit favorite.
Serves 8.

    1 seedless watermelon
    1 cup sparkling wine
    1 tablespoon fresh lemon juice
    ½ cup fresh blackberries
    Lemon peel

Cut watermelon into ½-inch round slices. Cut each slice into quarters to form triangles. Arrange slices on a serving platter. Combine sparkling wine and lemon juice in a small bowl. Sprinkle wine mixture over watermelon slices. Cover and refrigerate for at least 2 hours. Before serving, spoon juices that have collected in platter over fruit. Sprinkle blackberries over each serving of melon. Garnish with lemon peel.

Roasted Peach Tart

Serves 6 to 8.

Pâte Sable
    For recipe, see page 142.
Filling
    2⅓ cups milk
    1 vanilla bean
    2 eggs, at room temperature
    ½ cup granulated sugar
    2 tablespoons all-purpose flour
    2 tablespoons kirsch
    3 ripe peaches, skinned, halved, pitted, and thinly sliced
    1 tablespoon granulated sugar
    3 tablespoons currant jelly
    1 tablespoon kirsch

Prepare Pâte Sable pastry as directed.
    Scald milk with vanilla bean in a medium saucepan over medium heat. Whisk eggs and sugar together in a small bowl. Slowly whisk egg mixture into milk. Stir in flour. Reduce heat to low. Cook and stir constantly until mixture thickens and coats the back of a metal spoon. Remove from heat. Stir in 2 tablespoons kirsch. Cool completely.
    Pour milk mixture into prepared tart shell. Arrange peach slices on top. Sprinkle with 1 tablespoon granulated sugar. Broil until caramelized, about 5 minutes. Meanwhile, heat currant jelly in a small heat-proof dish until melted. Press jelly through a fine sieve. Stir in 1 tablespoon kirsch. Brush jelly mixture over peaches. Cover and refrigerate for at least 1 hour. To serve, remove tart rim and cut into wedges.

Citrus-Scented Poppy Seed Cake, Grilled Fruit Kabobs, and Lemon-Lime Summer Coolers

Mile-High Strawberry Pie with Chocolate-Orange Cookie Crust

Almost any combination of berries can be used in this dramatic mousse-filled pie.
Serves 8.

Chocolate-Orange Cookie Crust
1 cup all-purpose flour
¼ cup firmly packed light brown sugar
¼ cup unsweetened cocoa powder
1 tablespoon finely grated orange peel
½ cup unsalted butter, chilled and cut into pieces
1 to 2½ tablespoons fresh orange juice

Strawberry Filling
¼ cup fresh orange juice
1 envelope unflavored gelatin
1 egg, at room temperature
1 egg yolk, at room temperature
3 tablespoons granulated sugar
1 pint fresh strawberries, rinsed and hulled
1 tablespoon framboise
1⅓ cup whipping cream

Garnish
1 pint fresh strawberries, rinsed, hulled, and halved
1 whole strawberry, rinsed and hulled
½ cup red currant jelly
1 tablespoon framboise

For crust, preheat oven to 350°. Toss together flour, brown sugar, cocoa powder, and orange peel in a large bowl. Cut in butter with a pastry cutter or two knives used scissor-fashion until mixture resembles coarse crumbs. Sprinkle 1 tablespoon orange juice over mixture; toss with a fork. Add enough of remaining orange juice, one teaspoon at a time, tossing until mixture is just moistened. Pat dough onto bottom and up sides of a 9-inch pie plate. Flute edges of dough or fold them under and press with tines of a fork. Prick shell ½-inch apart over bottom and sides with a fork. Bake for 20 to 25 minutes or until lightly browned. Cool completely before filling.

For filling, place ¼ cup orange juice in top of a double boiler. Sprinkle gelatin over orange juice. Let mixture stand until liquid is absorbed, about 5 to 10 minutes.

Meanwhile, beat egg, egg yolk, and granulated sugar in a medium mixing bowl on medium-high speed until mixture is thick and forms a slowly dissolving ribbon when beaters are lifted, about 5 to 7 minutes; set aside.

Combine 1 pint strawberries and framboise in a food processor or blender and purée until smooth. Set top of double boiler with gelatin mixture over simmering water, stirring until gelatin completely dissolves. Remove from heat. Stir gelatin into egg mixture. Fold in puréed strawberry mixture. Beat whipping cream in a chilled bowl with chilled beaters until stiff. Fold whipped cream into strawberry mixture. Gently spoon strawberry mixture into prepared crust. Place plastic wrap directly onto filling's surface. Chill for at least 2 hours.

For garnish, carefully overlap 1 pint strawberry halves, cut side down, in concentric circles on top of filling. Place whole strawberry, stem side down, in center. Melt currant jelly in a small saucepan over low heat. Bring to a boil. Remove from heat; stir in 1 tablespoon framboise. Paint berries with currant glaze using a pastry brush. Loosely cover pie with plastic wrap. Chill pie for at least 4 hours or overnight.

Citrus Scented Poppy Seed Cake

Poppy seeds give off a light slate blue appearance when baked into this cake. It is perfect for summer entertaining since it can be frozen up 1 month in advance and transports exceptionally well.
Serves 10 to 12.

½ cup poppy seeds
½ cup milk
1½ cups unsalted butter, softened
1½ cups granulated sugar
2 tablespoons finely grated lemon peel
1 tablespoon finely grated orange peel
8 egg yolks, at room temperature
2 cups cake flour, sifted
¾ teaspoon salt
8 egg whites, at room temperature
Glaze
½ cup fresh lemon juice
¼ cup fresh orange juice
⅓ cup granulated sugar
Thinly sliced lemon
Thinly sliced orange

For cake, soak poppy seeds in milk in a small bowl for 4 hours; drain well. Grease and lightly flour a 12-cup fluted tube pan. Preheat oven to 350°.

Beat butter and 1½ cups sugar in a large mixing bowl on medium speed until light and fluffy. Beat in lemon peel and orange peel. Add drained poppy seeds. Add egg yolks, one at a time, beating well after each addition. Beat mixture until light and fluffy, about 5 minutes; set aside.

Stir together flour and salt. Fold flour mixture, one third at a time, into egg yolk mixture.

Beat egg whites in a large mixing bowl on high speed until stiff. Fold egg whites, one third at a time, into egg yolk batter. Gently pour batter into prepared pan. Bake for 50 to 60 minutes or until cake tester inserted into center comes out clean. Cool in pan for 5 minutes. Unmold cake into wire rack set over waxed paper.

For glaze, combine lemon juice, orange juice, and ⅓ cup sugar in a small bowl; stir until sugar dissolves. Pour juice mixture over warm cake until outside is moist but not soggy. Cool cake completely. Garnish with lemon slices and orange slices.

Grilled Fruit Kabobs

Dessert kabobs are the ideal dessert for a summer cookout because you can use the warm coals leftover from grilling your main dish meat.
Serves 8.

½ cup honey
½ cup unsalted butter
2 tablespoons lime juice
1 teaspoon ground cinnamon
Assorted fresh fruit, cut into chunks and pieces
8 wooden skewers, soaked in water to prevent burning

Make sure coals are warm. Combine honey, butter, lime juice, and cinnamon in a small heavy saucepan. Place on grill rack over warm coals. Stir until butter melts. Prepare kabobs by skewering alternate types of fresh fruit on skewers. Grill until lightly browned, about 3 to 5 minutes, brushing frequently with honey mixture. Turn fruit kabobs until all sides of fruit are tender. Serve warm.

Lemon-Lime Summer Coolers

Makes about 16 cups.

2 12-ounce cans frozen lime concentrate
2 12-ounce cans frozen lemonade concentrate
5 12-ounce cans water (use empty lime and lemonade containers)
1 one-fifth bottle light rum

Combine all ingredients in a large plastic freezer containers. Seal and freeze for at least 4 hours. Remove from freezer about 15 minutes before serving. Spoon mixture into tall glasses.

A Sensational Baby Shower

Brandied Boysenberry Cobbler
Frozen Chocolate Soufflé
Lemon Chiffon Cheesecake with Glazed Raspberries
Passion Fruit Iced Tea

Baby showers aren't just for women anymore! More and more of these celebrations now include the proud father-to-be, his family, and male friends. But with men at the party, planning your dessert menu becomes more important than ever.

My baby shower dessert party is perfect. I get rave reviews every time I serve my Brandied Boysenberry Cobbler. I think it finds a wonderful complement in the Lemon Chiffon Cheesecake with Glazed Raspberries, and the Frozen Chocolate Soufflé offers a good note of contrast in texture and color.

Decorate your table with baby toys—rattles, small stuffed animals, and blocks. Add silver heirloom pieces and, for a pretty finish, flowers in pastel colors.

Lemon Chiffon Cheesecake with Glazed Raspberries

Brandied Boysenberry Cobbler

Macaroon crumbs absorb and hold the brandied juices in this delicious cobbler.
Serves 6.

Topping
½ cup unsalted butter, softened
½ cup plus 1 tablespoon granulated sugar
1 egg
2½ teaspoons milk
1 teaspoon vanilla
1 cup plus 2 tablespoons all-purpose flour
1 teaspoon baking powder
¾ teaspoon finely grated lime peel

Filling
5 to 6 fresh boysenberries, rinsed
1 cup granulated sugar
⅓ cup brandy
1 tablespoon fresh lime juice
1¼ cups crushed macaroon cookie crumbs
¼ cup unsalted butter, melted
2 tablespoons granulated sugar

Vanilla Bean Ice Cream
For recipe, see page 61.

For topping, beat butter and ½ cup plus 1 tablespoon sugar in a small mixing bowl on medium speed until light and fluffy. Beat in egg, milk, and vanilla. Lower speed and add flour and baking powder. Beat till well combined. Stir in lime peel. Cover with plastic wrap and chill for 30 minutes.

For filling, combine boysenberries, 1 cup sugar, brandy, and lime juice in a medium bowl. Transfer fruit mixture to an oval 1½-quart baking dish. Combine macaroon crumbs and ¼ cup melted butter in a small bowl. Sprinkle crumbs over berries; set aside.

Preheat oven to 375°. Roll dough between two pieces of waxed paper into an oval the size of the baking dish. Remove top layer of waxed paper. Cut dough into a scalloped pattern, trimming 1 inch off the edge of the oval. Gently invert dough over berries. Remove remaining waxed paper. Sprinkle 2 tablespoons granulated sugar over top. Bake for 35 to 45 minutes or until filling is bubbly and crust is golden brown. Serve with Vanilla Bean Ice Cream.

Frozen Chocolate Soufflé

Chocolate, eggs, and whipping cream provide the basis for this luscious, simple to make frozen soufflé.
Serves 12 to 14.

½ cup finely chopped pistachio nuts
2 envelopes unflavored gelatin
⅔ cup crème de cacao liqueur
½ cup water
½ cup granulated sugar
2 cups bittersweet chocolate, coarsely chopped
8 egg yolks, at room temperature
8 egg whites, at room temperature
Pinch of salt
¾ cup granulated sugar
2 cups whipping cream

Make a collar for a 2-quart soufflé dish. Tear a piece of aluminum foil 4 to 6 inches longer than the dish's circumference. Fold foil in half lengthwise. Fit foil around the outside of the soufflé dish, extending 3 inches above the top, and secure with tape or a string tied 2 to 3 inches above the base of the dish. Butter inside of foil ring. Sprinkle chopped pistachios on collar.

For soufflé, sprinkle gelatin over crème de cacao and water in a heavy 2-quart saucepan; let stand for 5 minutes. Add ½ cup sugar to gelatin mixture and place over low heat. Cook, stirring constantly, until gelatin and sugar dissolve. Add chocolate; stir until melted. Remove from heat. Add egg yolks, one at a time, blending well after each addition. Cool completely.

Beat egg whites and salt in a large mixing bowl on medium-high speed until foamy. Gradually add ¾ cup sugar, beating until stiff. Gently fold egg whites, one third at a time, into cooled chocolate mixture. Beat whipping cream in a small chilled bowl with chilled beaters until stiff. Gently fold whipped cream into chocolate mixture. Spoon mixture into prepared soufflé dish. Freeze for 4 hours, or overnight.

To serve, carefully remove foil collar from dish. Serve immediately.

Lemon Chiffon Cheesecake with Glazed Raspberries

Serves 12.

Crust
  4 cups graham cracker crumbs
  ⅓ cup granulated sugar
  1 cup unsalted butter, melted

Filling
  ¼ cup ice water
  1 envelope unflavored gelatin
  ¾ cup granulated sugar
  5 egg yolks, at room temperature
  Pinch of salt
  ⅓ cup milk, scalded
  3 8-ounce packages cream cheese, softened
  ⅓ cup fresh lemon juice
  ¼ cup Grand Marnier
  2 teaspoons finely grated lemon peel
  ½ teaspoon vanilla
  5 egg whites, at room temperature
  ½ cup granulated sugar

Raspberry Glaze
  ¾ cup granulated sugar
  ¾ cup water
  3 tablespoons cornstarch
  2 tablespoons light corn syrup
  3 to 4 drops red food coloring (optional)
  3 to 4 cups fresh raspberries, rinsed

Preheat oven to 350°. For crust, stir together crumbs, ⅓ cup sugar, and melted butter in a large bowl. Press mixture onto bottom and up sides of a 10-inch springform pan. Bake for 12 minutes. Cool completely.

For filling, pour ¼ cup ice water into a cup. Sprinkle gelatin over water; let stand until softened, about 5 minutes. Combine ¾ cup sugar, egg yolks, and salt in top of a double boiler set over simmering water; cook and stir until sugar dissolves. Gradually add hot milk, beating constantly until thick, about 5 minutes. Add softened gelatin and stir until completely dissolved. Cool to lukewarm.

Beat cream cheese in a large mixing bowl on medium speed until smooth. Beat in 1 tablespoon egg yolk mixture, then fold in remaining yolk mixture. Fold in lemon juice, Grand Marnier, lemon peel, and vanilla. Beat egg whites in a large mixing bowl on medium-high speed until foamy. Gradually add ½ cup sugar and beat until stiff. Fold egg whites, one third at a time, into cream cheese mixture. Spoon filling into prepared crust. Cover with plastic wrap. Chill for 2 hours or until set.

For raspberry glaze, combine ¾ cup sugar, ¾ cup water, and cornstarch in a medium saucepan over medium-high heat. Cook and stir until mixture is thick and clear. Remove from heat. Stir in corn syrup and food coloring, if desired. Cool glaze until lukewarm. Arrange berries over chilled cheesecake. Pour glaze evenly over berries. Chill cheesecake for 6 hours or overnight.

A Summer Soirée

Blackberry Buttermilk Tart with
Blackberry-Peach Ice Cream
Nectarines in Red Wine with Zabaglione Cream
Raspberry Vodka Cordials
Assorted Dessert Cheeses

Enjoy summer's long days and cool evenings down to the last minute, since alfresco dining is soon to be a memory. As August schedules ease everyone seems to have a little extra time for entertaining. A Summer Soirée allows you and your guests to celebrate the season with a complement of desserts that require minimum cooking time and only uses the oven for one do-ahead tart.

The spectacle of a sunset provides the backdrop for this party whether the party is held at a summer home, the beach, on a boat, or on the veranda. This menu takes full advantage of the last of summer's wild blackberries, red raspberries, and juicy peaches and nectarines.

Nectarines in Red Wine and Raspberry Vodka Cordials

Blackberry Buttermilk Tart
with Blackberry-Peach Ice Cream

This sophisticated dessert makes the most of summer's black-berry harvest. I prefer to use large Pacific Northwest blackberries.
Serves 6 to 8.

Pâte Sable
  For recipe, see page 142.
Filling
  1 cup buttermilk
  3 large egg yolks
  ½ cup granulated sugar
  ¼ cup unsalted butter, melted and cooled
  2 tablespoons all-purpose flour
  1 tablespoon finely grated lemon peel
  1 tablespoon fresh lemon juice
  1 teaspoon vanilla
  ½ teaspoon salt
  2 cups fresh blackberries, rinsed
  Confectioners' sugar

Prepare Pâte Sable as directed.
  Meanwhile, prepare filling. Combine buttermilk, egg yolks, sugar, butter, flour, lemon peel, lemon juice, vanilla, and salt in a mixing bowl until smooth. Spoon blackberries evenly over bottom of baked pastry shell. Pour buttermilk mixture over blackberries. Bake for 30 to 35 minutes or until filling is set. Cool tart in pan on a wire rack. Remove tart rim. Dust with confectioners' sugar. Serve with Blackberry-Peach Ice Cream.

Blackberry-Peach Ice Cream

Makes about 2 quarts.

  2 cups diced peaches (about 3 medium peaches)
  1½ cups fresh blackberries, rinsed
  2 eggs, beaten
  ½ cup granulated sugar
  1 7-ounce jar marshmallow cream
  2 cups whipping cream
  1 cup half and half
  ¼ cup brandy

Purée peaches and blackberries in a blender or food processor. Press purée through a fine sieve; discard seeds.
  Combine beaten eggs, sugar, and marshmallow cream in a medium mixing bowl. Stir in whipping cream, half and half, brandy, and fruit purée. Cover and chill for at least 1 hour. Stir mixture. Transfer mixture into an ice cream canister. Prepare according to manufacturer's directions.

Nectarines in Red Wine with Zabaglione Cream

The unique characteristics of red wine and fresh nectarines offset and complement each other in this easy-to-prepare dessert. Any recipe that calls for nectarines can use peaches with equal aplomb. For best results, use slightly under ripe fruit for poaching.
Serves 6.

  6 large nectarines, peeled, halved, pitted, and sliced into
    ½-inch slices
  1 tablespoon fresh lemon juice
  2 cups dry red wine
  ¼ cup granulated sugar
  1 cinnamon stick
  2 tablespoons brandy
Zabaglione Cream
  3 egg yolks
  ¼ cup granulated sugar
  ⅓ Grand Marnier
  ½ cup whipping cream
  1 tablespoon confectioners' sugar
  1 pint fresh raspberries (optional)

Sprinkle nectarine slices with lemon juice. Set aside.
Combine wine, ¼ cup granulated sugar, and cinnamon stick in a medium saucepan over medium-high heat. Bring mixture to a boil. Reduce heat to low and add nectarine slices to mixture. Poach nectarines until tender, about 5 to 8 minutes. Remove from heat. Transfer fruit to a separate bowl using a slotted spoon. Cool nectarines and liquid separately. Arrange nectarines in a deep glass serving bowl. Stir brandy into reserved liquid. Pour liquid over fruit. Cover with plastic wrap and refrigerate for at least 4 hours.
For Zabaglione Cream, whisk together egg yolks and ¼ cup granulated sugar in top of a double boiler until light and fluffy. Slowly whisk in Grand Marnier. Set double boiler over simmering water, whisking constantly until mixture thickens enough to coat the back of a metal spoon, about 5 minutes. Do not boil. Remove from heat. Whisk mixture until cool, about 2 to 3 minutes. Cover with plastic wrap so that plastic touches surface of mixture. Refrigerate for 1 hour.

Meanwhile, beat whipping cream with confectioners' sugar in a chilled bowl with chilled beaters until stiff. Fold whipped cream mixture into egg yolk mixture. Cover and chill until ready to serve with nectarines.
To serve, spoon nectarines into a serving dish. Dollop with Zabaglione Cream. Serve with raspberries if desired.

Raspberry Vodka Cordials

For best results, plan ahead, since this recipe improves with age. A cordial will keep indefinitely if stored in a cool, dark place. It makes a beautiful and festive holiday gift.
Makes 8 cups.

  6 cups fresh raspberries, rinsed
  3 cups granulated sugar
  3 cups vodka
  2 cups brandy

Place raspberries and sugar in a 4-quart glass jar. Pour vodka and brandy over berry mixture. Cover jar with a secure fitting lid. Place jar in a cool dark place for 1 to 2 months, stirring the cordial weekly. Strain finished cordial through a fine sieve lined with a damp cheesecloth into a decanter.

6
Elegant Autumn Parties

European Dessert Soirée
Back to School Brunch
Oktoberfest
Tricks or Treats
New Orleans Fête
After Theatre Rendezvous

European Dessert Soirée

Nüss Tart
Cassata al Cioccolata
Palmiers
Black Forest Cheesecake
Austrian Apple Strudel
Viennese Layer Bars
Espresso Bar

Europe's pastry shops have always been a source of both decorative and culinary inspiration. Who can walk down the streets of any town or village in France, Germany, Italy, or Austria without finding cakes, tortes, pastries, and strudels in fascinating shapes, colors, and flavors? This menu was inspired by memories of eating my way through konditories, boulangeries, and pastisseries while sipping on cappuccino or espresso.

Magically transport your guests overseas with a dessert buffet laden with European delicacies such as a rich Nüss Tart, flakey French Palmiers, Viennese Layer Bars (reminiscent of flavors from the famous Sacher Torte and Linzertorte), Austrian Apple Strudel, Germany's Black Forest Cheesecake, Italy's Cassata al Cioccolata (layers of pound cake laced with amaretto and filled with ricotta cheese and chocolate and frosted with chocolate), and of course espresso.

With such an abundance of goodness, the buffet table automatically becomes the center of attention. Set the table with lace or white linen, china dessert plates, silver, and candles. An adjoining table can offer an espresso bar. Set the mood by playing Mozart softly in the background.

Black Forest Cheesecake, Viennese Layer Bars, and Espresso

Nüss Tart

Nüss (which means "nut") Tart can be prepared two days in advance and refrigerated. Bring to room temperature before serving.
Serves 8 to 10.

Pastry
⅔ cup finely gound almonds or hazelnuts
1¼ cups all-purpose flour, sifted
½ cup cake flour, sifted
⅓ cup granulated sugar
1 tablespoon finely grated lemon peel
½ cup unsalted butter, chilled and cut into pieces
1 egg yolk
2 to 4 tablespoons milk

Filling
1 cup coarsely chopped walnuts or hazelnuts
⅔ cup granulated sugar
⅔ cup half and half
2 tablespoons dark rum
¼ teaspoon ground cinnamon
⅛ teaspoon ground cloves
⅛ teaspoon ground nutmeg
⅓ cup seedless raspberry jam

Rum Glaze
½ cup confectioners' sugar
1 tablespoon light rum
2 to 4 tablespoons half and half

Garnish
1 cup whipping cream
3 tablespoons confectioners' sugar
1 tablespoon dark rum
Confectioners' sugar

Butter and lightly flour a 9-inch tart pan with removable bottom. For pastry, toss together almonds or hazelnuts, all-purpose flour, cake flour, ⅓ cup granulated sugar, and lemon peel in a bowl. Cut in butter using a pastry blender or two knives used scissor-fashion until mixture resembles coarse crumbs. Add egg yolk; blend well (mixture will be crumbly). Add milk, one tablespoon at a time, until dough can be formed into a ball. Break off two thirds of dough. Press

dough onto bottom and up sides of prepared tart pan. With hands, form remaining dough into a ball. Place ball between two sheets of waxed paper. Slightly flatten ball with hands. Roll pastry from center to edges into a 10-inch circle. Transfer pastry circle to a baking sheet. Refrigerate dough while preparing filling.

For filling, combine walnuts or hazelnuts, granulated sugar, ⅔ cup half and half, 2 tablespoons dark rum, cinnamon, cloves, and nutmeg in a heavy, 2-quart saucepan over low heat. Cook, stirring constantly, until sugar dissolves. Increase heat to high. Boil gently until mixture thickens, about 5 to 7 minutes; stir occasionally. Cool completely.

Preheat oven to 350°. Spread raspberry jam over bottom of tart pastry. Pour filling over raspberry jam in tart shell. Remove top sheet of waxed paper over pastry circle. Invert pastry circle over filling. Remove remaining wax paper. Gently press top and bottom pastry together to seal. Place tart on a baking sheet. Bake for 35 to 40 minutes, or until golden brown. Cool.

For glaze, combine ½ cup confectioners' sugar, 1 tablespoon light rum, and 2 tablespoons half and half in a small bowl. Add enough additional half and half, to achieve a glaze of drizzling consistency. Drizzle over cooled tart.

For garnish, beat whipping cream, 3 tablespoons confectioners' sugar, and 1 tablespoon dark rum in a chilled bowl with chilled beaters until stiff. Chill until ready to use.

To assemble, remove tart from pan. Garnish tart with whipped cream mixture.

Cassata Al Cioccolata

Dried cherries replace glacéed cherries to update this classic Italian favorite. A store-bought pound cake will give you a head start on this recipe.
Serves 12.

Pound Cake
  1 cup unsalted butter, softened
  2 cups confectioners' sugar, sifted
  3 eggs, at room temperature
  1½ cups flour
  ½ teaspoon vanilla
Syrup
  ¼ cup water
  ¼ cup granulated sugar
  ¼ cup amaretto
Filling
  4 ounces dried cherries, coarsely chopped
  ¼ cup amaretto
  1 15- or 16-ounce container ricotta cheese
  ¼ cup granulated sugar
  ⅓ cup semi-sweet chocolate chips
  ⅓ cup finely chopped blanched almonds
Frosting
  2 cups semi-sweet chocolate chips
  1 cup unsalted butter, softened and cut into 12 pieces
  ¾ cup amaretto
  Slivered almonds, for garnish

For pound cake, grease and flour a 9 × 5½-inch loaf pan. Preheat oven to 350°. Beat 1 cup butter in a large mixing bowl on medium speed. Slowly add confectioners' sugar, beating until light and fluffy. Add eggs, one at a time, blending well after each addition. Reduce speed to low and add flour, one cup at a time, blending well after each addition. Increase speed to medium and beat for 7 minutes. Add vanilla. Pour batter into prepared loaf pan. Bake for 50 to 60 minutes, or until a cake tester inserted in center comes out clean. Cool in pan for 5 minutes. Remove from pan by inverting loaf onto a wire rack. Cool completely before filling. Cut a thin slice of cake off top to level using a serrated knife; trim cake so it is even on all sides and perfectly straight. Slice cake horizontally into 3 even layers; set aside.

For syrup, combine water and ¼ cup granulated sugar in a heavy, 2-quart saucepan over medium heat. Cook, stirring constantly, until sugar dissolves. Remove from heat; stir in ¼ cup amaretto. Set aside.

For filling, soak cherries in ¼ cup amaretto for 30 minutes. Stir together ricotta cheese and ¼ cup granulated sugar in a small bowl until smooth. Fold in ⅓ cup chocolate chips and almonds. Fold in cherry and amaretto mixture.

For frosting, melt 2 cups chocolate chips in top of a double boiler set over simmering water, stirring until smooth. Remove from heat. Whisk in 1 cup butter, one piece at a time, beating until smooth. Place pan with chocolate mixture in a bowl filled with ice water. Continue whisking until mixture thickens. Gradually whisk in ¾ cup amaretto. Whisk until mixture is of spreading consistency.

To assemble, place bottom slice of cake, cut side up, on a serving plate. Brush slice with one third of syrup. Spread with one half of filling. Cover with second cake layer. Repeat procedure, ending with third layer. Press gently with hands so layers adhere. Spread frosting over top and sides of cake. Sprinkle slivered almonds over top. Freeze cake for 30 minutes, or chill thoroughly in refrigerator until frosting is set, about 2 hours. Cover cake loosely with plastic wrap. Refrigerate for 24 hours or more. If desired, reserve ¾ cup chocolate frosting and pipe garnish around base and top.

Note: Dried cherries are available in specialty food shops or can be ordered by mail from American Spoon Foods, 1-800-222-5886.

Tip: Pound cake freezes well for up to 2 months.

Palmiers

Known to many as palm leaves or elephant ears, these familiar French cookies are made of puff pastry. For minimum effort, use a high-quality store-bought puff pastry.
Makes 3 dozen.

1 pound sheet puff pastry, chilled
   (For recipe, see page 141.)
1⅓ cups granulated sugar

Prepare puff pastry as directed in recipe or thaw according to package directions.

Cut a sheet of parchment paper or aluminum foil into a 16-inch square. Sprinkle ½ cup of the granulated sugar over square. Place puff pastry on top. Sprinkle another ½ cup sugar over pastry. Using a lightly floured rolling pin, evenly roll dough into 14-inch, ½-inch thick square. Transfer paper and pastry onto a baking sheet. Refrigerate until well chilled, about 15 minutes. Using a well-floured sharp knife, trim ⅛- to ¼-inch from each edge. Fold two opposite sides of square into center, leaving a 1-inch gap in middle. Fold again to bring folded edges together. The pastry should now have 4 distinct layers. Cover and refrigerate until chilled, about 30 minutes.

Cover a baking sheet with parchment paper or aluminum foil. Place remaining ⅓ cup sugar in a shallow dish. Using a well-floured sharp knife, cut pastry roll into ¾-inch slices. Dip cut sides of each slice into sugar. Place each slice 2 inches apart on prepared baking sheet. Cover with plastic and refrigerate until chilled, about 15 minutes. Preheat oven to 375°. Bake for 20 minutes or until golden on top. Carefully turn over each cookie with a wide spatula; bake for an additional 5 minutes or until golden brown. Transfer cookies to a wire rack. Cool completely.

Black Forest Cheesecake

In this rendition of the famous Black Forest Cake, chocolate, cherries, and whipped cream create a rich and beautiful dessert.
Serves 12.

Cherry Topping
1 16-ounce can pitted tart cherries, drained (reserve juice)
¼ cup kirsch
2 tablespoons granulated sugar
2 tablespoons cornstarch
1 tablespoon reserved cherry juice
¼ teaspoon red food coloring (optional)

Chocolate Crumb Crust
2½ cups chocolate cookie crumbs
½ cup granulated sugar
½ cup unsalted butter, melted

Filling
12 ounces bittersweet chocolate, coarsely chopped
3 8-ounce packages cream cheese, softened
1 cup granulated sugar
3 eggs, at room temperature
1 cup sour cream
1 tablespoon kirsch
1 teaspoon vanilla

Topping
1 cup whipping cream
3 tablespoons confectioners' sugar
1½ tablespoons kirsch

For topping, soak cherries in ¼ cup kirsch in a bowl for 3 hours or overnight. Drain cherries; reserve kirsch. Combine 2 tablespoons granulated sugar and cornstarch in a cup. Stir in 1 tablespoon reserved cherry juice and if desired, red food coloring. Add drained cherries, stirring to coat. Let mixture stand for 1 hour.

Strain cherries, pouring liquid into a small heavy saucepan. Cook liquid, stirring constantly, until mixture becomes very thick. (When the cherries are added the mixture will thin out.) Fold in cherries with a rubber spatula, and cook, stirring occasionally, until mixture is once again thick. Remove from heat; cool completely.

For crust, combine chocolate cookie crumbs, ½ cup granulated sugar, and melted butter in a 10-inch springform pan;

mix until well blended. Press mixture onto the bottom and 1½ inches up sides of pan. Refrigerate until ready to use.

Preheat oven to 350°. For filling, melt chocolate in top of a double boiler set over simmering water, stirring until smooth. Remove from heat. Beat together cream cheese and 1 cup granulated sugar in a large mixing bowl on medium speed until light and fluffy. Add eggs, one at a time, blending well after each addition. Beat in melted chocolate, sour cream, 1 tablespoon kirsch, and vanilla; blend until smooth. Spoon filling into crust. Bake for 1 hour or until cheesecake is just firm when pan is gently shaken. Cool cheesecake on a wire rack; do not remove metal ring from springform pan. Cover and refrigerate cheesecake overnight.

For topping, beat whipping cream and confectioners' sugar in a chilled bowl with chillled beaters until stiff.

To assemble, remove metal ring from springform pan. Spread cherries over cheesecake. Pipe whipped cream mixture into rosettes around top edge of cake. Chill until ready to serve.

Austrian Apple Strudel

Strudel is best served warm from the oven when the leaves of phyllo dough are still flakey and crisp. Strudels can be filled with nearly any variety of fresh or dried fruit and nut combination.
Makes 8 servings.

  3 large tart green apples, peeled, cored, and cut into
      ⅛-inch slices
  2 tablespoons fresh lemon juice
  Peel from 1 lemon, finely grated
  ½ cup granulated sugar
  ½ cup chopped walnuts
  ¼ cup raisins or dried currants
  1½ teaspoons ground cinnamon
  ¼ teaspoon ground cardamom
  ¼ teaspoon ground cloves
  ¼ teaspoon ground ginger
  6 sheets phyllo pastry (defrosted if frozen)
  ¾ cup clarified butter, melted *
  ⅓ cup white bread crumbs
  ⅓ cup granulated sugar
  Confectioners' sugar

Toss sliced apples, lemon juice, lemon peel, ½ cup granulated sugar, walnuts, raisins or currants, cinnamon, cardamom, cloves, and ginger in a large bowl; set aside.

Grease a 15½ × 10½ × 1-inch jelly roll pan. Preheat oven to 400°. Place a slightly damp cloth on the counter. Place two phyllo leaves on cloth, long side facing you. Brush with melted butter. Toss together bread crumbs and ⅓ cup granulated sugar in a small cup. Sprinkle each sheet with 2 tablespoons crumb and sugar mixture. Place two more sheets on top and repeat procedure. Follow with remaining phyllo, melted butter, and crumb-sugar mixture.

Spread apple filling over bottom third of pastry, leaving a 1½-inch border. Discard any remaining liquid in bowl. Fold narrow ends of phyllo over filling; seal well, using a little of the remaining butter, if necessary. Starting with the longer end, using the cloth as a guide, gently roll strudel up jelly-roll fashion. Place seam side down on prepared baking sheet. Brush strudel with remaining butter. Bake for 25 to 35 minutes, or until golden brown. Sift confectioners' sugar over strudel. Serve warm or at room temperature.

* To clarify butter, melt butter in a saucepan over low heat. Do not brown. Set aside for a few minutes. Skim the white sediment from the top and pour off the golden liquid into a jar. Discard any white sediment remaining on the pan's bottom. Clarified butter will keep refrigerated for two to three weeks.

Note: To freeze strudel, butter a double thickness of foil. Place unbaked strudel on prepared foil, and wrap it tightly. Freeze. Do not defrost; unwrap and place frozen strudel on a greased jelly roll pan. Bake in a preheated 375° oven for 35 to 40 minutes, or until golden brown.

Viennese Layer Bars

Makes about 5 dozen.

Nut Filling
6 cups finely ground pecans
¾ cup granulated sugar
1 teaspoon ground cinnamon

Pastry
5 cups all-purpose flour
1 cup plus 2 tablespoons granulated sugar
1 tablespoon baking soda
2½ teaspoons baking power
1¼ cups unsalted butter, chilled and cut into 1-inch pieces
5 egg yolks
⅓ cup plus 1 tablespoon sour cream
2 tablespoons rum
1 tablespoon vanilla
1 cup seedless red raspberry preserves
1¼ cups apricot preserves
1 egg white

For filling, combine pecans, ¾ cup sugar, and cinnamon in a bowl; set aside.

For pastry, combine flour, 1 cup plus 2 tablespoons sugar, baking soda, and baking powder in a large bowl. Cut in butter using a pastry cutter or two knives scissor-fashion until mixture resembles coarse crumbs. Whisk egg yolks, sour cream, rum, and vanilla in a small bowl until blended. Pour egg mixture over flour mixture. Blend until mixture forms a ball.

Preheat oven to 350°. Grease a 10 × 15-inch jelly roll pan. Divide pastry into 3 equal pieces. Roll out 1 piece of dough between 2 sheets of wax paper to a 10 × 15-inch rectangle. Place dough into prepared pan; discard wax paper. Trim pastry edges. Spread raspberry preserves over pastry. Lightly press 2¼ cups nut filling into preserves. Roll out second piece of pastry as described above. Place over nut mixture. Remove paper. Top with apricot preserves and follow with 2¼ cups nut filling. Roll out last piece of dough and place over nut filling. Beat egg white in a cup with a fork until foamy. Brush egg white over top of pastry dough. Evenly sprinkle with remaining nut mixture. Pat nuts lightly to secure. Bake for 35 minutes or until a cake tester inserted in center comes out clean. Cool completely in pan. Cover and let stand overnight before serving. Cut into 1-inch squares. Store in an airtight container.

Note: Viennese Layer Bars can be made 5 days ahead and stored at room temperature or frozen for 2 months.

Back to School Brunch

Peanut Butter and Jelly Rolls
Asian Fruit Platter with Ginger Dip
Dutch Baby with Apple Compote
Pear and Jarlsberg Cheese Breakfast Soufflé
Hot Autumn Toddy

t's back to school time, that special time of year that marks the close of summer and the beginning of fall. With it comes the opportunity to renew acquaintances and friends lost during the summer, as well as to join family together before students leave home for school. A Back to School Brunch welcomes the change of seasons and the resumption of busy schedules with a menu that incorporates the distinctive flavors of fall: tart green apples, sweet pears, peanut butter and jelly, and hot spiced beverages are traditional parts of autumn fare.

Just as the foilage has changed to shades of red, gold, and rust, the table has turned to warm colors and bold geometric forms. Colorful ceramics in autumn hues complement the season and the food.

Peanut Butter and Jelly Rolls

Try this updated version of the timeless peanut butter and jelly sandwich.
Makes 1 dozen.

Sweet Yeast Dough
   3 cups all-purpose flour
   ¼ cup granulated sugar
   1 package active dry yeast
   ⅔ cup milk
   2 tablespoons butter, softened
   1 egg, beaten

Filling
   2 tablespoons butter, melted
   ¾ cup creamy peanut butter
   ⅓ cup raspberry jam or desired berry jam
   ½ cup coarsely chopped peanuts

Generously grease a large bowl; set aside. For dough, stir together 1½ cups flour, sugar, and yeast in a large mixing bowl. Heat milk with 2 tablespoons butter in a small, heavy saucepan over medium heat until mixture reaches 115°. Slowly beat warmed milk mixture into flour mixture on low speed until well blended. Increase speed to medium and beat for 2 minutes. Add beaten egg. Beat in 1 cup flour with a spoon until smooth. Mix in enough of remaining ½ cup flour to make a soft dough. Turn dough onto a lightly floured surface and knead for about 10 minutes or until smooth and elastic. Place dough into prepared bowl, turning once to grease top. Let dough rise in a warm, draft-free place until double, about 1½ hours.

Grease a 13 × 9 × 2-inch baking pan; set aside. Punch dough down. Roll dough out to a 17 × 12-inch rectangle on a lightly floured surface. For filling, brush surface of dough with 2 tablespoons melted butter and spread with peanut butter and jam; sprinkle with peanuts. Starting with the larger end, roll up dough jelly-roll fashion. Cut into twelve equal rolls. Arrange rolls, cut sides up, in prepared pan. Cover and let rise in a warm, draft-free place until double, about one hour.

Preheat oven to 375°. Bake for 25 to 30 minutes, or until lightly browned. Serve warm or cool.

Peanut Butter and Jelly Rolls, Dutch Baby with Apple Compote, Asian Fruit Platter with Ginger Dip, and Hot Autumn Toddies

Asian Fruit Platter with Ginger Dip

Serves 6 to 8.

   ¼ cup granulated sugar
   ¼ cup sherry vinegar
   2 tablespoons sesame seeds, toasted
   1 tablespoon finely grated fresh ginger root
   1 tablespoon honey
   1 teaspoon dry mustard
   1 teaspoon paprika
   ½ teaspoon salt
   ¾ cup vegetable oil
   Assorted fresh fruits, washed and sliced

Whisk together sugar, vinegar, sesame seeds, ginger root, honey, mustard, paprika, and salt until sugar dissolves. Slowly pour oil into ginger mixture, whisking constantly until oil is absorbed and dressing is thickened. Refrigerate, tightly covered, until ready to serve.

To serve, arrange fruits on a serving tray. Pour dressing into a small bowl and serve alongside fruit.

Dutch Baby with Apple Compote

Also known as a German pancake, a Dutch Baby can be served dusted with confectioners' sugar, a slice of lemon, and pure maple syrup.
Serves 6.

Dutch Baby
2 tablespoons unsalted butter, melted
6 eggs
1 cup all-purpose flour
2 tablespoons granulated sugar
½ teaspoon salt
1 cup milk

Apple Compote
6 tablespoons unsalted butter
3 large Golden Delicious apples, peeled, cored, and
  coarsely chopped
1 cinnamon stick, broken in half
½ cup granulated sugar
6 tablespoons applejack (optional)
¼ cup apple juice
½ teaspoon fresh lemon juice
Confectioners' sugar
Lemon slices

Preheat oven to 400°. For Dutch Baby, brush 2 table-spoons melted butter over entire surface of a 10-inch dutch baby pan or a 10-inch nonstick, oven-proof skillet. Beat eggs slightly in a large mixing bowl. Beat in flour, 2 tablespoons granulated sugar, and salt on low speed. Gradually add milk. Increase speed to medium-high and beat until smooth. Pour batter into prepared pan. Bake for 15 minutes. Reduce oven temperature to 325°. Bake for 40 to 45 minutes longer, or until golden brown and puffy. Immediately loosen pancake from pan and slide onto serving plate.

For Apple Compote, melt 4 tablespoons butter in a heavy skillet over medium-high heat. Add apples and cinnamon stick and cook for 5 minutes. Sprinkle with ½ cup granulated sugar. Cook until apples are tender and juices turn golden, stirring frequently, about 8 to 10 minutes. Remove from heat and add applejack, if desired, and apple juice. Return to heat and bring to a boil. Remove from heat and mix in remaining 2 tablespoons butter and lemon juice.

Fill baked Dutch Baby with warm Apple Compote. Dust with confectioners' sugar. Garnish with lemon slices. Serve immediately.

Pear and Jarlsberg Cheese Breakfast Soufflé

Make ahead and refrigerate until ready to serve. This soufflé is equally delicious served for lunch or as an accompaniment to a pork or chicken dinner.
Serves 6.

2 tablespoons butter, melted
8 Bosc pears, peeled, cored, and thinly sliced
¾ cup light brown sugar, firmly packed
1½ teaspoons pumpkin pie spice
¼ cup butter, melted
4 eggs, lightly beaten
1 cup all-purpose flour
1½ cups shredded Jarlsberg cheese
¼ teaspoon salt

Preheat oven to 350°. Brush 2 tablespoons melted butter over bottom of 9-inch square baking pan. Arrange pear slices in pan. Sprinkle brown sugar and pumpkin pie spice over pears. Bake for 20 minutes.

Stir together ¼ cup melted butter, eggs, flour, cheese, and salt in a medium bowl; pour over hot pears. Bake for 25 to 30 minutes, or until puffy and golden brown. Serve immediately.

Hot Autumn Toddy

The butter mixture can be made one day ahead, covered, and refrigerated.
Serves 6.

¼ cup unsalted butter, softened
1½ tablespoons triple sec or orange liqueur
1 cup dark brown sugar, firmly packed
¼ teaspoon ground cinnamon
Pinch of freshly grated nutmeg
Pinch of ground cloves
Pinch of ground allspice
3 cups boiling water
18 tablespoons bourbon
6 slices lemon

Beat butter and triple sec or orange liqueur in a small mixing bowl on medium speed, beating until smooth. Add brown sugar, cinnamon, nutmeg, cloves, and allspice, beating until smooth.

To serve, place 2 tablespoons butter mixture into six 6-ounce heat-proof glasses or mugs. Add ½ cup boiling water and 3 tablespoons bourbon to each; stir until smooth. Garnish each with a lemon slice. Serve hot. (Save remaining batter for future use.)

Oktoberfest

Cheddar Cheesecake with Spiced Pear Topping
Individual Pumpkin Charlottes
Orange-Scented Cranberry and Black Walnut Cake
Figs with Mascarpone
Chocolate-Painted Leaf Cookies

Fall's the time for those rousing, wonderful food festivals that celebrate autumn's abundance. Let the finest seasonal produce—apples, plums, pears, pumpkins, cranberries, and nuts—offer inspiration for a fall festival of your own.

This Oktoberfest party menu offers both familiar flavors and wonderful surprises, and the combination of fruit, nuts, cinnamon, spices, and cheese gives you fresh approaches to autumn classics.

Don't limit the bounty of the harvest to the food alone. Incorporate the colors of autumn into your table setting. Place colorful ceramic dishes on woven or ragged-edge place mats. Offset these ceramics with antique silverware or country-style stainless steel and simple glassware. Use miniature pumpkins, colorful gourds, and assorted nuts to decorate the table. Celebrate the joy of the season!

Cheddar Cheesecake with Spiced Pear Topping, Individual Pumpkin Charlottes, and Chocolate-Painted Leaf Cookies

Cheddar Cheesecake with Spiced Pear Topping

The classic combination of cheese and fruit works wonderfully in this savory cheesecake.
Serves 12.

Crust
1 cup all-purpose flour
¼ cup granulated sugar
½ teaspoon finely grated lemon peel
½ cup unsalted butter, chilled and cut into 1-inch pieces
2 egg yolks, lightly beaten
½ teaspoon vanilla

Filling
4 8-ounce packages cream cheese, softened
1½ cups (6 ounces) grated cheddar cheese
1½ cups granulated sugar
3 tablespoons cornstarch
6 eggs, at room temperature
¼ cup sour cream
¼ cup beer, at room temperature

Spiced Pear Topping
3 cups Bosc pears, peeled, cored, and sliced
½ cup unsweetened apple juice, divided
¼ cup granulated sugar
¼ teaspoon ground cinnamon
1 tablespoon cornstarch
½ teaspoon vanilla

Garnish
Lemon peel
Orange peel

Preheat oven to 400°. For crust, combine flour, ¼ cup sugar and ½ teaspoon lemon peel in a medium bowl. Cut butter into flour mixture using a pastry blender or two knives used scissor-fashion, until mixture resembles coarse crumbs. Add beaten egg yolks and ½ teaspoon vanilla; mix well. Press mixture onto the bottom and up the sides of a 9- or 10-inch springform pan. Bake for 5 minutes. Set aside until ready to fill.

Reduce oven temperature to 325°. For filling, beat together cream cheese and cheddar cheese in a large mixing bowl on medium speed until smooth. Add 1½ cups sugar and 3 tablespoons cornstarch; beat until smooth. Add eggs, one at a time, blending well after each addition. Stir in sour cream and beer. Pour filling into prepared crust. Bake for 1 hour. Turn off oven. Cool cheesecake completely in oven with door slightly ajar.

For pear topping, poach sliced pears in ¼ cup of the apple juice until crisp-tender. Do not overcook. Remove from heat and add ¼ cup sugar and cinnamon, stirring until sugar dissolves. Stir together 1 tablespoon cornstarch and remaining ¼ cup apple juice in a cup; pour over apple slices. Add ½ teaspoon vanilla. Return pear mixture to medium heat and cook until clear and thick, stirring occasionally. Remove from heat. Cool completely. Arrange pear slices on top of cheesecake. Spoon remaining glaze over pears. Cover and chill overnight. To serve, remove metal ring from springform pan. Garnish with additional lemon and orange peel.

Individual Pumpkin Charlottes

Serves 10.

Crust
- 28 3½-inch ladyfingers, store-bought or homemade (For recipe, see page 141.)
- ¼ cup butter, melted
- 2 tablespoons Frangelico or hazelnut liqueur
- ½ cup ground gingersnap cookies

Filling
- 1 cup milk
- ½ cup light brown sugar, firmly packed
- 4 egg yolks
- 2 envelopes unflavored gelatin
- 1 16-ounce can unsweetened solid pack pumpkin
- 2 teaspoons finely grated orange peel
- ½ teaspoon ground ginger
- ¼ teaspoon ground nutmeg
- ¼ teaspoon ground cloves
- 1 cup whipping cream
- ⅓ cup granulated sugar
- ½ cup Frangelico or hazelnut liqueur
- 4 egg whites, at room temperature

Topping
- 10 whole hazelnuts, coarsely chopped
- 1 tablespoon granulated sugar
- ⅛ teaspoon ground ginger
- ⅛ teaspoon ground nutmeg
- Pinch of ground cloves

Garnish
- ½ cup whipping cream
- 4½ teaspoons Frangelico or hazelnut liqueur
- 1 tablespoon confectioners' sugar

For crust, butter ten ⅔-cup ceramic soufflé dishes or ramekins. Line bottom of dishes with waxed paper. Cut ladyfingers in half crosswise. Mix together melted butter and 2 tablespoons Frangelico in a small bowl. Brush sides of ladyfingers with butter mixture. Sprinkle flat side of ladyfingers with gingersnaps. Line sides of molds with ladyfingers, cut end up and rounded side out; set aside.

For filling, combine milk, brown sugar, egg yolks, and gelatin in a heavy 2-quart saucepan over low heat, stirring constantly until thick. Remove from heat. Stir in pumpkin, orange peel, ½ teaspoon ginger, ¼ teaspoon nutmeg, and ¼ teaspoon cloves; blend well. Beat 1 cup whipping cream and ⅓ cup granulated sugar in a chilled bowl with chilled beaters until stiff. Fold ½ cup Frangelico into whipped cream. Beat egg whites in a large mixing bowl on high speed until stiff peaks form. Gently fold egg whites, one third at a time, into pumpkin mixture. Fold in whipped cream. Pour mixture into prepared soufflé dishes. Cover and refrigerate for 6 hours or overnight.

For topping, grease a baking sheet. Combine chopped hazelnuts, 1 tablespoon granulated sugar, ⅛ teaspoon ginger, ⅛ teaspoon nutmeg, and pinch of cloves in a small skillet over low heat until sugar melts and coats hazelnuts, stirring occasionally. Turn hazelnuts out onto prepared cookie sheet. Cool; separate pieces.

For garnish, beat ½ cup whipping cream, 4½ teaspoons Frangelico, and confectioners' sugar in a chilled bowl with chilled beaters until stiff.

To serve, dip dishes or ramekins in hot water for several seconds to loosen charlottes. Invert onto individual serving dishes. Peel off waxed paper. Spoon whipped cream into a pastry bag fitted with a star tip. Pipe rosettes decoratively over top and in rows between ladyfingers. Sprinkle spiced hazelnuts over top.

Orange-Scented Cranberry and Black Walnut Cake

Black walnuts give this cake an unusual earthy flavor, but if you can't find them at your local specialty food store, use ordinary walnuts.
Serves 10.

2½ cups cake flour
1 tablespoon baking powder
¾ teaspoon baking soda
½ teaspoon ground cloves
½ teaspoon ground nutmeg
¼ teaspoon salt
1½ cups granulated sugar
1 cup coarsely chopped black walnuts
1 cup whole fresh cranberries
4 teaspoons grated orange peel
3 eggs, beaten
1¼ cups vegetable oil
½ cup orange juice concentrate
½ cup sour cream

Orange Glaze
2 cups confectioners' sugar
3 tablespoons orange juice concentrate, thawed
2 tablespoons water
½ teaspoon vanilla

Candied Orange Peel Garnish
2 large thick-skinned oranges
½ cup granulated sugar
2 tablespoons grenadine

Grease and flour a 12-cup fluted cake pan; set aside. Preheat oven to 350°.

Sift together cake flour, baking powder, baking soda, cloves, nutmeg, and salt in a large bowl. Add 1½ cups granulated sugar, walnuts, cranberries, and orange peel. Combine eggs, oil, ½ cup orange juice concentrate, and sour cream in a small bowl. Add orange mixture to dry ingredients, mixing thoroughly. Pour into prepared pan. Bake for 50 to 55 minutes or until a cake tester inserted in center comes out clean. Cool in pan for 10 to 15 minutes; invert onto a wire rack.

For glaze, stir together confectioners' sugar, 3 tablespoons orange juice concentrate, water, and vanilla in a small bowl until smooth. Spoon glaze over top of warm cake, allowing some to drizzle down sides. Cool completely before serving.

For garnish, cut peel away from oranges into 1-inch wide strips using a vegetable peeler. Cut away white pith from peel. Cut peel into 3-inch long, ⅛-inch wide strips. Blanch peel in a small saucepan of boiling water for 1 minute. Drain; rinse peel under cool water.

Combine peel, ½ cup granulated sugar, and grenadine in a heavy saucepan over low heat, stirring occasionally until sugar dissolves and peel is translucent, about 15 to 20 minutes. Drain completely. Transfer peel to a waxed paper-lined plate, separating each piece to prevent sticking. Cool completely. Sprinkle orange peel over glaze. (Can be prepared up to 1 week in advance. Store in a tight container at room temperature.)

Note: Orange-Scented Cranberry and Black Walnut Cake can be prepared 3 days in advance.

Figs with Mascarpone

Serves 8.

8 ounces mascarpone cheese
16 to 24 figs, sliced in half
Hazelnuts, coarsely chopped

Beat mascarpone cheese in a small bowl until smooth. Put cheese into small crocks. Arrange fig halves on a serving plate. Garnish with chopped hazelnuts. Serve with a small knife for spreading cheese onto figs.

Chocolate-Painted Leaf Cookies

Beautiful cookies for a special occasion.
Makes about 60 4-inch cookies.

1 7-ounce tube almond paste
¾ cup confectioners' sugar
3 egg whites, at room temperature
¼ cup cake flour
Pinch of salt
1 tablespoon whipping cream
6 ounces bittersweet chocolate

Line baking sheets with parchment paper; set aside. Preheat oven to 350°. Beat almond paste and confectioners' sugar in a large mixing bowl at medium speed until mixture resembles coarse crumbs. Add egg whites, one at a time, beating until smooth. Fold in flour and salt. Stir in whipping cream.

Place metal leaf stencil on parchment paper. Spread a very thin layer of batter, about ¹⁄₁₆-inch thick, across leaf using narrow metal spatula. Carefully lift stencil. Repeat with remaining batter. Bake for 8 to 10 minutes, or until edges are golden brown. Cool cookies; then peel from paper.

Melt chocolate in top of a double boiler set over simmering water, stirring until smooth. Spread a thin layer of chocolate on one half of the cookie lengthwise, or pour melted chocolate into pastry bag fitted with a small round decorator tip and pipe free-form designs on each cookie. Let chocolate cool until set.

Note: Metal leaf stencils can be ordered by mail from Maid of Scandinavia. Call 1-800-328-6722 (Minnesota residents, call 1-800-851-1121) for a catalog.

You can make a leaf stencil out of a thin heavy cardboard by tracing a leaf pattern, about 4 × 2-inches, onto the cardboard and carefully cutting out the shape.

Tricks or Treats

English Toffee Cake
Pizza Pan Cookie
Cobweb Peanut Butter Cup Pie
Old-Fashioned Caramel Apples
Popcorn Butter Crunch
Ghost, Ghoul, and Goblin Sugar Cookies

Everyone—young and old—loves a Halloween party! Set the mood by turning your home into a haunted house, complete with dimly lit halls, cobwebs, skeletons, and eerie music. Cover the buffet table with a cloth in the classic burnt orange and black colors of the holiday. Carved pumpkins and black cats make festive centerpieces.

The favorite treats found in Halloween bags are incorporated in this menu: English Toffee Cake, Popcorn Butter Crunch, and Cobweb Peanut Butter Pie. Save time and energy by setting up different stations for mini-gremlins to dip their own caramel apples and decorate their own haunted cookies. Don't forget to fill a caldron with apple cider!

Cobweb Peanut Butter Cup Pie with Ghost, Ghoul, and Goblin
Sugar Cookies

English Toffee Cake

This candy-studded cake creates a wonderful combination of taste, texture, and color.
Serves 8 to 10.

2½ cups all-purpose flour, sifted
2 teaspoons baking soda
2 teaspoons baking powder
¼ teaspoon salt
1 cup unsalted butter, softened
1⅓ cups granulated sugar
4 eggs, at room temperature
2 teaspoons vanilla
2 cups sour cream
6 ounces English toffee candy bars (i.e., Heath Bars), frozen and broken into bite-size pieces

Vanilla Glaze
1 cup confectioners' sugar
2 to 3 teaspoons milk
½ teaspoon vanilla
1 tablespoon light corn syrup
English toffee candy bars, crushed (optional)

Grease and flour a 12-cup fluted cake pan; set aside. Preheat oven to 325°. Combine flour, baking soda, baking powder, and salt in a bowl; set aside. Beat butter and granulated sugar in a large mixing bowl on medium speed until light and fluffy. Add eggs, one at a time, blending well after each addition. Add 2 teaspoons vanilla. Alternately add flour mixture and sour cream to butter mixture, beginning and ending with flour. Pour one third of batter into prepared pan. Sprinkle with 3 ounces crushed toffee. Pour another one third of batter over candy. Sprinkle remaining crushed toffee over batter. Top with remaining batter. Bake for 55 to 60 minutes or until a cake tester inserted in center comes out clean. Cool in pan for 15 minutes. Turn cake out onto a wire rack. Cool completely.

For Vanilla Glaze, combine confectioners' sugar, 2 teaspoons milk, ½ teaspoon vanilla, and corn syrup in a small bowl; stir until smooth. Add additional milk if necessary to make glaze drizzling consistency. Drizzle glaze over cooled cake. Garnish with additional candy, if desired.

Pizza Pan Cookie

Leslie Cohen created this warm-from-the-oven pizza-shaped cookie topped with marshmallows, peanuts, and chocolate.
Serves 10 to 12.

1 cup unsalted butter, softened
½ cup granulated sugar
½ cup firmly packed brown sugar
1 egg
2 teaspoons vanilla
1½ to 1¾ cups all-purpose flour
1½ cups semi-sweet chocolate chips
1½ cup roasted peanuts
2 cups miniature marshmallows

Grease and flour a 12-inch round pizza pan. Preheat oven to 350°. Cream together butter and sugars. Add egg and vanilla; beat well. Stir in flour. Spread dough evenly in pan. Bake for 20 minutes or until golden brown and firm in center. Combine chocolate, peanuts, and marshmallows in a bowl. Sprinkle evenly over hot cookie. Return to oven. Bake for 15 minutes or until marshmallows are golden brown. Cool for about 10 minutes. Cut into 10 to 12 wedges. Serve warm.

Cobweb Peanut Butter Cup Pie

An irresistably rich, no-bake dessert.
Serves 8 to 10.

Crust
  1½ cups chocolate cookie crumbs
  2 tablespoons granulated sugar
  ¼ teaspoon ground cinnamon
  ⅓ cup unsalted butter, melted

Filling
  1 8-ounce package cream cheese, softened
  1 cup creamy peanut butter
  1 cup granulated sugar
  2 tablespoons unsalted butter, melted
  1 tablespoon vanilla
  1 cup whipping cream
  ¼ cup chopped peanuts

Topping
  1 cup semi-sweet chocolate chips
  ½ cup whipping cream
  3 to 4 ounces vanilla-flavored candy coating, broken into
    pieces

For crust, toss together cookie crumbs, 2 tablespoons sugar, and cinnamon in a 9-inch pie plate. Pour ⅓ cup melted butter over crumbs; mix until well blended. Press mixture onto the bottom and sides of pie plate. Chill until ready to fill.

For filling, beat cream cheese in a medium mixing bowl on medium speed until fluffy. Beat in peanut butter. Gradually add 1 cup sugar. Add 2 tablespoons melted butter and vanilla; beat well. Beat whipping cream in a chilled bowl with chilled beaters until stiff. Fold whipped cream, one third at a time, into peanut butter mixture. Gently spoon mixture into prepared pie shell. Sprinkle peanuts over top. Cover and refrigerate.

Meanwhile, for topping, melt chocolate chips with whipping cream in top of a double boiler set over simmering water, stirring until smooth. Remove from heat. Melt candy coating in a cup set in simmering water, stirring until smooth. Spoon candy coating into a pastry bag fitted with a small round pastry tip. Spread semi-sweet chocolate mixture over filling. Pipe candy coating in concentric circles over semi-sweet chocolate. Using the tip of a sharp knife, pull white chocolate through semi-sweet chocolate, starting from center moving out to edge of pie plate. Repeat to form a cobweb effect. Chill pie for at least 4 hours or overnight.

Old-Fashioned Caramel Apples

Serves 8.

  8 wooden sticks
  8 medium apples
  2 cups granulated sugar
  1 cup firmly packed brown sugar
  1 cup whipping cream
  ⅔ cup butter
  Pinch of salt
  2 teaspoons vanilla

Grease a baking sheet. Insert a wooden stick into the stem end of each apple; set aside. Combine sugar, brown sugar, whipping cream, butter, and salt in a heavy medium saucepan over medium-low heat, stirring constantly until sugar dissolves. Increase heat to medium-high and bring mixture to a boil. Cook until a candy thermometer reaches 225°. Remove from heat. Stir in vanilla.

Holding onto the stick, dip each apple into the hot caramel, turning until coated. Scrape off excess caramel. Place apple on prepared baking sheet. Repeat with remaining apples. (If caramel becomes too thick, heat mixture gently over low heat until it reaches the desired consistency.) Let apples sit until caramel hardens, about 10 minutes.

Popcorn Butter Crunch

This pecan, caramel, and popcorn mixture makes a terrific holiday snack for kids and adults. It can be stored in an airtight container for 3 days, but chances are it won't last that long.
Makes about 14 cups.

1½ cups pecan halves, toasted
10 cups popped unsalted popcorn
1 cup granulated sugar
1 cup unsalted butter
¼ cup light corn syrup
2 tablespoons maple syrup

Grease a 15½ × 10½ × 1-inch jelly roll pan; set aside. Grease a large bowl. Toss together pecans and popcorn in prepared bowl. Combine sugar, butter, corn syrup, and maple syrup in a heavy 2-quart saucepan. Cook over medium-high heat, stirring constantly until mixture reaches 225° on a candy thermometer. Pour over popcorn mixture, stirring to coat. Spread on prepared jelly roll pan. Cool completely. Break candy into pieces.

Ghost, Ghoul, and Goblin Sugar Cookies

Makes about 2 dozen 4-inch cookies.

1 cup unsalted butter, softened
1 cup granulated sugar
2 eggs
1 tablespoon vanilla
3 cups all-purpose flour
1 tablespoon baking powder
Buttercream Frosting
6 tablespoons unsalted butter, softened
3 cups confectioners' sugar, sifted
4 to 6 teaspoons milk
½ teaspoon vanilla
Assorted food coloring (optional)

Beat 1 cup butter and granulated sugar in a medium mixing bowl on medium speed until light and fluffy. Add eggs and 1 tablespoon vanilla. Beat until well combined. Add flour and baking powder; beat on low speed until well combined. Chill dough for 1 hour.

Preheat oven to 350°. Form dough into a ball. Slightly flatten ball with hands on a lightly floured surface. Using a well-floured rolling pin, evenly roll dough from center to edges until ¼-inch thick. Cut dough using assorted Halloween-shaped cookie cutters. Place cookies 1 inch apart on ungreased cookie sheets. Bake for 10 minutes, or until light golden at edges. Transfer cookies to wire racks. Cool completely before frosting. Decorate with frosting, if desired.

For Buttercream Frosting, beat together 6 tablespoons butter and confectioners' sugar in a medium mixing bowl on medium speed until smooth. Beat in 4 teaspoons milk and ½ teaspoon vanilla. Add additional milk, one teaspoon at a time, until frosting is of spreading consistency. Divide frosting into batches and add food coloring, if desired. Place frosting in a pastry bag fitted with a small round or small star decorating tip. Pipe frosting in assorted patterns on cookies.

Note: Sugar Cookies freeze well for up to 2 months.

New Orleans Fête

Beignets
Chocolate Pecan Tassies
Bourbon Street Bread Pudding
Café Brulot

Visitors to New Orleans learn that there are three principal topics of discussion: food, food, and food. Good food, and lots of it, is second nature to Louisianians. Happy hour in New Orleans lasts from dusk to dawn. Perhaps the fact that New Orleans is below sea level, and by all rights should be under water, gives everyone who lives in New Orleans a daily reason to celebrate. Some of the best desserts of the South are found in the French Quarter, Garden District, the Old French Market and on Bourbon Street.

Cane syrup, molasses, and brown sugar were once staples of the Southern kitchen. Today corn syrup has replaced cane, and commercially processed white and brown sugars have replaced molasses and brown sugar crystals. Bread pudding and pecan pie are favorites. In New Orleans, some of life's finest pleasures are also life's simplest. The satisfying combination of beignets and café brulot is one of them.

The hour for this party doesn't have to be at the end of the day. It could be a late evening party, a Sunday afternoon garden party, or a Mardi Gras celebration. Invite your guests to sample the sweets of New Orleans.

Beignets

I was inspired by a visit to Café Du Monde in New Orleans to recreate these light French doughnuts. Beignets (pronounced ben-YAYS) are best served hot.
Makes about 2 dozen.

  1 cup milk
  2 tablespoons shortening
  2 tablespoons granulated sugar
  1 package active dry yeast
  3 cups all-purpose flour, sifted
  1 teaspoon ground nutmeg
  1 teaspoon salt
  1 egg
  6 cups vegetable oil for deep-fat frying
  Confectioners' sugar

Heat milk and shortening in a small, heavy saucepan over medium heat until mixture reaches 115°. Combine sugar and yeast in a large bowl. Slowly beat warm milk mixture into sugar mixture, stirring until sugar dissolves. Stir together flour, nutmeg, and salt in a bowl. Add 1 cup flour mixture to milk mixture, stirring until smooth. Beat in egg. Gradually add remaining flour mixture, occasionally scraping sides of bowl, mixing until smooth. (Dough will be stiff.) Cover and set in a warm, draft-free place until double, about 1 hour.

Roll dough out to ⅛-inch thickness on a lightly floured surface. Using a sharp knife, cut dough into 2-inch squares. Place squares 2 inches apart on ungreased baking sheets. Cover and allow dough to double, about 1 hour.

Heat oil to 370°. Carefully drop dough into hot oil. Cook until golden brown, turning once. Remove from oil using a slotted spoon. Drain on paper towels. Generously dust beignets with confectioners' sugar. Repeat procedure with remaining dough. Serve hot.

Chocolate Pecan Tassies

Make these bite-size tartlets 1 to 2 months in advance. Store them in an airtight container in the freezer.
Makes 2 dozen.

Crust
  ½ cup unsalted butter, softened
  1 3-ounce package cream cheese, softened
  1 cup all-purpose flour
Filling
  1 1-ounce square unsweetened chocolate
  1 egg
  ¾ cup firmly packed light brown sugar
  ½ cup chopped pecans
  2 tablespoons unsalted butter, softened
  ¼ teaspoon vanilla
  Pinch of salt
Garnish
  1 cup whipping cream
  ¼ cup confectioners' sugar
  ¼ teaspoon rum extract

For crust, beat together butter and cream cheese in a small mixing bowl on medium speed until smooth. Beat in flour. With floured hands, divide dough into 24 equal pieces. Press dough onto the bottom and sides of 24 small ungreased muffin tins or small decorative tart pans. Refrigerate until ready to fill.

Preheat oven to 350°. For filling, melt chocolate in a cup set in simmering water, stirring until smooth. Remove from heat. Cool. Beat egg with brown sugar in a small bowl until smooth. Stir in pecans, butter, vanilla, and salt. Stir in melted chocolate. Fill prepared muffin tins. Bake for 25 minutes or until filling is slightly puffed and the crust is golden brown. Cool in tins on a wire rack.

For garnish, beat whipping cream, confectioners' sugar, and rum extract in a small chilled bowl with chilled beaters until stiff. Dollop tarts with whipped cream mixture just before serving.

Chocolate Pecan Tassies, Bourbon Street Bread Pudding, and Café Brulot

Bourbon Street Bread Pudding

Cardamom lends a delicious nuance to this Southern dessert. *Serves 10.*

Bread Pudding
1½ tablespoons unsalted butter, melted
12 1-inch thick slices stale French bread
2 cups half and half
2 cups milk
2 cups granulated sugar
6 eggs
½ cup unsalted butter, softened
1 tablespoon vanilla
1½ cups raisins
2 teaspoons grated orange peel
½ teaspoon ground cinnamon
1 teaspoon ground cardamom
Bourbon Sauce
¾ cup granulated sugar
1 egg
½ cup unsalted butter, melted
1 to 3 tablespoons water
Pinch of ground cinnamon
½ to ¾ cup bourbon

For bread pudding, grease a 9-inch square baking pan or dish with 1½ tablespoons melted butter. Preheat oven to 350°. Break bread into 1-inch pieces; place in a large bowl. Stir together half and half, milk, 2 cups sugar, 6 eggs, ½ cup butter, vanilla, raisins, orange peel, ½ teaspoon cinnamon, and cardamom in a medium bowl. Pour milk mixture over bread; let stand until bread absorbs most of moisture, about 10 to 15 minutes. Pour mixture into prepared pan. Set baking pan into a roasting pan. Pour enough simmering water to come within ½ inch of top of baking pan (this water bath technique is known as a *bain marie*). Cover and bake for 50 minutes or until pudding is set but not firm. Uncover and bake for 10 minutes or until light golden brown. Cool.

For Bourbon Sauce, mix together ¾ cup sugar and 1 egg in a small bowl. Add ½ cup melted butter, stirring until sugar dissolves. Add water, 1 tablespoon at a time, to aid in dissolving sugar if necessary. Stir in a pinch of cinnamon. Stir in bourbon.

Spoon Bourbon Sauce over pudding. Place pan under broiler until brown and bubbly. Remove immediately. Serve warm or at room temperature.

Note: Bread Pudding can be made up to two days in advance. Pour Bourbon Sauce over pudding just before serving. Broiling is optional. For single servings, place pieces of pudding on individual, oven-proof serving dishes. Spoon Bourbon Sauce over pudding; broil.

Café Brulot

Impress your guests with this flaming beverage. *Serves 8.*

8 tablespoons brandy
Peel of 1 orange, julienned
Peel of 1 lemon, julienned
2 2-inch cinnamon sticks
8 whole cloves
2 tablespoons granulated sugar
3 cups hot strong coffee

Heat brandy, orange peel, lemon peel, cinnamon sticks, cloves, and sugar in a heavy, 2-quart saucepan or in top of chafing dish or café brulot bowl over low heat. Tilt pan and ignite brandy (optional). When flame subsides, stir until sugar dissolves. Stir in hot coffee. Serve in café brulot or demitasse cups.

After Theatre Rendezvous

Flaming Hazelnut Purses Filled
with Dried Fruit and Nuts
Cognac or Brandy

t has been said that good things come in small packages. Wrapped, ignited, and sauced, Hazelnut Purses Filled with Dried Fruit and Nuts are a spectacular finale to a special evening with friends. Although crêpes are easy to prepare, they provide the basis for a dramatic, make-ahead dessert. Nothing needs to accompany this show-stopping dessert except snifters filled with warmed brandy or cognac and perhaps a selection of fruit and cheese.

Hazelnut Purses Filled with Dried Fruit and Nuts

The key to successful flambéing (from the French word *flamber,* "to flame") is to use spirits that are at least 80 proof. *Makes 15 to 20 crêpes.*

Crêpes
1 Hazelnut Crêpe recipe, see page 143.

Maple Crème Anglaise
1 Maple Crème Anglaise recipe, see page 140.

Filling
1½ cups milk
⅔ cup granulated sugar
¼ cup plus 2 tablespoons honey
2 tablespoons unsalted butter
½ cup chopped dried apricots
¼ cup plus 2 tablespoons golden raisins
2 teaspoons finely grated lemon peel
1 tablespoon finely grated orange peel
3 cups finely ground skinned hazelnuts
1 cup fresh white cake crumbs or bread crumbs
½ teaspoon vanilla

Garnish
10 3 × ¼-inch strips of orange peel
10 3 × ¼-inch strips of lemon peel
¾ cup Grand Marnier

Prepare crêpe batter as directed; refrigerate until ready to use.

Prepare Maple Crème Anglaise as directed.

For filling, combine 1½ cups milk, sugar, honey, and butter in a medium saucepan over medium heat until simmering, stirring constantly until sugar dissolves. Stir in apricots, raisins, lemon peel, and orange peel. Add hazelnuts and cake or bread crumbs. Bring mixture to a boil, stirring constantly. Stir in ½ teaspoon vanilla. Remove from heat and cover until ready to use.

For garnish, blanch orange peel and lemon peel in a small saucepan of boiling water until limp, about 5 minutes. Remove peel from water; drain completely on paper towels. Cool completely. Set aside.

Cook crêpes as directed.

Preheat oven to 350°. Butter a shallow baking dish or oven-proof serving platter. To assemble, place each crêpe on a work surface so that golden side is down. Spoon about 2 tablespoons filling in center of each crêpe. Bring edges toward center like a sack and tie each sack with one strip of orange or lemon peel (a second pair of hands is helpful). Put crêpes on the prepared pan or platter. Bake until just heated through, about 5 minutes.

To serve, warm Grand Marnier in a small saucepan over low heat. Bring warm liqueur to table with crêpes. Ignite the Grand Marnier and pour over crêpes. Spoon some Maple Crème Anglaise onto each plate. Once flames subside, top with a crêpe purse. Serve immediately.

Flaming Hazelnut Purses Filled with Dried Fruit and Nuts

7
Festive Winter Parties

A Nutcracker Tea
A Tree Trimming Get-Together
New Year's Resolution Party
Super Bowl Sunday Brunch
Fireside Desserts for Two
Fondue Fantasy

A Nutcracker Tea

Swedish Thumbprint Cookies
Vanilla Pretzels
Butter Pecan Acorns
Antique Lace Rolls
Peppermint Fudge Brownies
Kourambiedes
Eggnog

Everyone loves cookies and the winter holiday season lends itself to baking. This simple, do-ahead tea menu incorporates a selection of international favorites with some contemporary variations on traditional themes. Eggnog replaces tea as the beverage served at this party. Join family and friends for A Nutcracker Tea after a matinee performance of the Nutcracker ballet or Dicken's *A Christmas Carol,* a busy day shopping, or a holiday open house.

Swedish Thumbprint Cookies, Vanilla Pretzels, Butter Pecan Acorns, Antique Lace Rolls, Peppermint Fudge Brownies, and Eggnog

Swedish Thumbprint Cookies

Makes 2½ dozen.

1 cup all-purpose flour
½ cup unsalted butter, softened
¼ cup firmly packed light brown sugar
½ teaspoon vanilla
¼ teaspoon salt
1 egg yolk
1 egg white
1 cup finely chopped walnuts
⅓ cup red currant jelly or other fruit jelly

Preheat oven to 350°. Combine flour, butter, brown sugar, vanilla, salt, and egg yolk in a small mixing bowl. Beat at low speed until smooth. Increase speed to medium; beat for 1 minute. Shape dough into ¾-inch balls. In a cup, beat egg white until foamy. Place nuts in a shallow dish. Dip balls of dough into egg white then roll in chopped nuts. Place cookies on an ungreased baking sheet. Make a ½-inch indention with thumb in center of each cookie. Bake for 15 minutes or until golden brown. Cool cookies on waxed paper. Spoon jelly into center of each cookie. Store cookies in an airtight container.

Vanilla Pretzels

These cookies freeze exceptionally well.
Makes about 3 dozen.

3½ cups all-purpose flour, sifted
1 cup granulated sugar
1 teaspoon baking powder
1 cup unsalted butter, cut into pieces
1 egg, lightly beaten
1 teaspoon vanilla
½ cup whipping cream
1 egg, lightly beaten
½ cup finely chopped unblanched almonds
3 tablespoons granulated sugar

Mix together flour, 1 cup granulated sugar, and baking powder into a large bowl. Cut in butter using a pastry blender or two knives used scissor-fashion until mixture resembles coarse crumbs. Combine 1 egg, vanilla, and whipping cream in a small bowl. Add cream mixture to flour mixture; blend well. (It may be necessary to use your fingers to completely work the ingredients together.) Gather dough up into a ball. Wrap dough in waxed paper and refrigerate for 30 minutes.

Grease baking sheets. Preheat oven to 325°. Break dough into quarter size pieces. Roll each piece into a long thin rope with floured hands. Shape dough into a pretzel. Arrange cookies on prepared baking sheets. Chill for 30 minutes. Brush cookies with remaining beaten egg using a pastry brush. Sprinkle chopped almonds over cookies. Bake for 25 minutes or until golden brown.

Butter Pecan Acorns

This is an easy yet elegant butter pecan cookie shaped to resemble an acorn.
Makes 3 dozen.

1 cup unsalted butter, melted
¾ cup firmly packed light brown sugar
¾ cup finely chopped pecans
1 teaspoon vanilla
2½ cups all-purpose flour
½ teaspoon baking powder
6 ounces bittersweet chocolate, chopped
¾ cup finely chopped pecans

Preheat oven to 375°. Beat together butter, brown sugar, ¾ cup pecans, and vanilla in a medium mixing bowl on medium speed. Decrease speed to low; add flour and baking powder. Beat until well combined. Shape dough into 1-inch balls. Slightly flatten by pressing bottom of ball onto ungreased baking sheet. Pinch tops of cookies to resemble acorns (see photograph). Bake for 10 to 12 minutes or until lightly golden. Remove cookies and cool on wire racks.

Melt chocolate in top of a double boiler set over simmering water, stirring until smooth. Remove from heat; keep double boiler over water. Place remaining ¾ cup pecans in a shallow dish. Dip large ends of cookies into melted chocolate then into pecans. Set cookies on waxed paper. Cool until chocolate is set.

Antique Lace Rolls

These pretty, fragile cookies require precision timing but are worth the effort. For a change, leave cookies flat and spread a thin layer of melted chocolate on the bottom of one cookie. Then press another cookie, bottom side down, on top to form sandwiches.
Makes about 2 dozen.

1 cup quick-cooking oatmeal
½ cup unsalted butter, melted
½ cup firmly packed light brown sugar
⅓ cup all-purpose flour
¼ cup finely chopped crystalized ginger
2 tablespoons milk

Lightly grease and flour baking sheets; set aside. Preheat oven to 350°. Combine oatmeal, melted butter, brown sugar, flour, ginger, and milk. Drop batter by teaspoonfuls 2 inches apart onto prepared baking sheets. Flatten cookies slightly with the back of a spoon. Bake for 7 to 9 minutes or until lightly browned. Cool for 1 minute or until edge is just firm enough to lift with a thin spatula. Then, working quickly, lift cookies and turn them top side down onto paper towels. Roll cookies over the handle of a wooden spoon to get a cylinder shape. Cool until crisp. If cookies get too firm to roll, warm them for a few minutes in the oven to soften. Store cookies in an airtight container.

Peppermint Fudge Brownies

These brownies are delicious on their own, but when combined with a cream cheese frosting and crushed peppermint candies, they are delectable.
Makes about 3 dozen.

2 cups semi-sweet chocolate chips
⅔ cup unsalted butter
4 eggs, at room temperature
1 cup granulated sugar
1 teaspoon vanilla
½ cup all-purpose flour, sifted
1 teaspoon baking powder
½ cup coarsely chopped pecans
1 cup semi-sweet chocolate chips
Cream Cheese Frosting
3 cups confectioners' sugar
1 3-ounce package cream cheese, softened
¼ cup unsalted butter, softened
6 to 8 tablespoons milk
½ cup crushed hard peppermint candy
Whole peppermint candies (optional)

Grease a 13 × 9 × 2-inch baking pan; set aside. Preheat oven to 350°. Melt 2 cups chocolate chips and ⅔ cup butter in top of a double boiler set over simmering water, stirring until smooth. Remove from heat. Beat together eggs and granulated sugar in a medium mixing bowl on medium speed. Add vanilla. Blend in melted chocolate mixture. Lower speed, and add sifted flour and baking powder; blend well. Fold in nuts and remaining 1 cup chocolate chips. Pour batter into prepared pan. Bake for 25 minutes. Cool completely.

For frosting, beat together confectioners' sugar, cream cheese, ¼ cup butter, and 4 tablespoons milk in a large mixing bowl on medium speed until smooth. Add additional milk, one tablespoon at a time, to achieve desired spreading consistency. Stir in crushed peppermint candy. Spread topping over cooled brownies. Cut into bars. Top each brownie with additional peppermint candy, if desired.

Kourambiedes

Kourambiedes (koo-ram-pe-A-thees) are Greek cookies flavored with cloves, brandy, and almond extract. The clove symbolizes the spices the Wise Men brought to the Christ child.
Makes 2 dozen.

½ cup unsalted butter, softened
⅓ cup confectioners' sugar
1 egg yolk, at room temperature
1 teaspoon brandy
½ teaspoon vanilla
¼ teaspoon almond extract
1½ cups all-purpose flour
24 whole cloves
Confectioners' sugar

Preheat oven to 350°. Beat butter in a small mixing bowl on medium speed until light and fluffy. Sift ⅓ cup confectioners' sugar over butter; mix well. Beat in egg yolk, brandy, vanilla, and almond extract. Beat flour into butter mixture. Divide dough into 4 equal parts. Make 6 balls out of each section. Arrange balls of dough on ungreased baking sheets. Stick a clove into top of each cookie. Bake for 18 minutes or until light brown. Transfer cookies to a wire rack set over waxed paper. Generously sift confectioners' sugar over warm cookies.

Eggnog

Serves 6.

6 egg yolks
1 cup granulated sugar
2 cups milk
1¼ cups brandy
⅓ cup dark rum
1½ tablespoons vanilla
6 egg whites, at room temperature
Pinch of salt
1 cup whipping cream
Freshly ground nutmeg

Beat egg yolks in a large mixing bowl on medium-high speed until pale. Gradually add sugar, beating until thick and pale. Beat in milk, brandy, rum, and vanilla.

Beat egg whites and salt in a large mixing bowl on high speed until stiff. Gently fold beaten egg whites, one third at a time, into egg yolk mixture.

Beat whipping cream in a chilled bowl with chilled beaters until stiff. Fold whipped cream into egg mixture. Chill for 3 hours or overnight.

Just before serving, gently stir eggnog. Pour eggnog into mugs; sprinkle with freshly ground nutmeg.

A Tree Trimming Get-Together

Steamed Chocolate Pudding with Persimmon Coulis
Ginger Ice Cream
Candied Pecans
Chocolate Cranberry Truffles

O' Tannenbaum, O' Tannenbaum. The Germans are responsible for immortalizing the Christmas tree not only in song but since their fifth-century mystery plays. Known as the "Paradise Tree" found in the midst of the Garden of Eden, the Christmas tree symbolized the coming of Christ. Originally the tree was decorated with apples and white wafers, representing sin and the salvation of the Blessed Sacrament.

Today, every family has its own tradition about selecting and decorating a Christmas tree. A Tree Trimming Get-Together with friends will become a perfect addition to your holiday tradition. Here decorations don't only grow on trees, but also trim the table.

This menu is built around a rich Steamed Chocolate Pudding set off by a bright Persimmon Coulis. With comforting hot drinks and a crackling fire, what a wonderful way to start off the season!

Steamed Chocolate Pudding with Persimmon Coulis and Ginger Ice Cream

Steamed Chocolate Pudding with Persimmon Coulis

George Morrone, a talented chef from Campton Place in San Francisco, and Bradley Ogden with the Bel Air Hotel in Los Angeles, created this elegant holiday dessert. Take a little extra time to duplicate the cocoa and confectioners' sugar checkerboard like it's done in the Bel Air dining room. The applause will be well worth the effort.
Serves 8 to 10.

1 cup unsalted butter, softened
⅓ cup granulated sugar
2 eggs
3 egg yolks
⅓ cup milk
⅓ cup whipping cream
1 teaspoon vanilla
6 ounces bittersweet chocolate, coarsely chopped
½ cup cake flour
1 teaspoon baking powder
½ teaspoon salt
1 cup milk
Confectioners' sugar
Unsweetened cocoa powder

Persimmon Coulis
4 very ripe persimmons
6 tablespoons confectioners' sugar
3 to 4 tablespoons fresh lime juice
2 tablespoons Grand Marnier

Line bottom of a 9-inch springform pan with parchment paper. Use about ¼ cup of the butter to grease paper; set aside. Preheat oven to 350°.

Beat remaining butter and granulated sugar in a medium mixing bowl on medium speed for 10 minutes. Add eggs; beat till well combined.

Combine egg yolks, ⅓ cup milk, whipping cream, and vanilla in top of a double boiler set over simmering water. Cook until mixture coats the back of a metal spoon, stirring occasionally. Remove from heat. Stir chocolate into hot mixture until smooth. Cool.

Add chocolate mixture to butter mixture; beat till well combined. Sift together flour, baking powder, and salt into a bowl. Alternately add flour mixture and 1 cup milk to chocolate mixture, beginning and ending with flour mixture. Pour into prepared pan. Set pan in a roasting pan. Pour in enough boiling water to reach halfway up the sides of the springform pan. Bake for 60 to 70 minutes, or until set and firm to the touch.

Cool for 10 minutes. Remove ring from springform pan. Cool completely. Remove parchment paper from bottom of pudding before decorating and serving.

To decorate, cut 3 or 4 strips of parchment or waxed paper about 12 inches long and 1½ inches wide. Place 3 of the paper strips across the top of the pudding about 1½ inches apart. Dust whole pudding with confectioners' sugar using a tea strainer. Carefully lift strips of paper off pudding, being careful not to get any of the confectioners' sugar on the open spaces of the pudding. Rotate pudding 180 degrees. Carefully place strips criss-crossing the confectioners' sugar so some of the pudding and some of the powdered sugar is exposed. Dust pudding with cocoa powder using a tea strainer. Carefully remove strips. The final result is a checkerboard design.

For Persimmon Coulis, halve the persimmons and spoon out the flesh. Remove any seeds. Process persimmon pulp, 6 tablespoons confectioners' sugar, lime juice, and Grand Marnier in a food processor or blender until smooth.

To serve, place pudding slice on a serving plate. Spoon 2 tablespoons Persimmon Coulis onto plate in a small circle next to pudding. Add scoop of Ginger Ice Cream adjacent to purée and pudding.

Ginger Ice Cream

A simple and delicious accompaniment to the Steamed Chocolate Pudding with Persimmon Coulis. For a summertime treat, pour hot fudge sauce over scoops of Ginger Ice Cream for a memorable sundae.
Makes about 1½ quarts.

2 cups skim or nonfat milk
1 1-inch piece peeled, sliced, fresh ginger root
7 egg yolks
1 cup granulated sugar
¼ cup finely minced fresh ginger root
1 cup whipping cream

Combine milk and sliced ginger in a heavy, 3-quart saucepan over medium heat. Bring to a boil. Remove from heat; strain ginger from milk. Beat egg yolks and sugar in a medium bowl until sugar is dissolved. Whisk warm milk and minced ginger root into egg yolk mixture. Pour mixture into top of a double boiler set over simmering water; cook until mixture thickens, whisking constantly. Remove from heat. Whisk in whipping cream. Chill for at least 2 hours. Transfer mixture to an ice cream canister. Prepare according to manufacturer's directions.

Candied Pecans

Used extensively in Chinese cooking, Chinese five-spice powder consists of equal parts of finely ground anise pepper, star anise, cassia or cinnamon, cloves, and fennel seed. It imparts a subtle flavor and is widely available in the Asian food section of most supermarkets or specialty grocery stores.
Makes about 4 cups.

4 cups pecan halves
½ cup granulated sugar
1 teaspoon Chinese five-spice powder
4 cups vegetable oil for deep-fat frying
Salt

Place pecans in a medium saucepan. Add enough boiling water to cover. Cook over medium-high heat for 30 seconds. Immediately drain pecans in a colander. Spread pecans on paper towels and pat dry. Place warm pecans in a large bowl.
Combine sugar and five-spice powder in a small bowl. Sprinkle sugar mixture over warm pecans; toss to coat thoroughly. Spread sugared pecans on a large baking sheet. Let stand, uncovered, at room temperature for at least 8 hours or overnight. Store at room temperature in an airtight container.

Chocolate Cranberry Truffles

Makes about 1½ dozen.

¼ cup whipping cream
2 ounces bittersweet chocolate, chopped
1 tablespoon unsalted butter
2 teaspoons Grand Marnier
¼ cup water
½ cup granulated sugar
20 whole fresh cranberries
½ cup ground toasted hazelnuts
Decorative candy papers

Heat whipping cream in a heavy saucepan over medium-low heat until small bubbles appear around the edges of the pan. Stir in chopped chocolate, stirring until smooth; remove from heat. Stir in butter and Grand Marnier. Pour chocolate mixture into a bowl and refrigerate, covered, for at least 2 hours.

Meanwhile, in a medium saucepan over medium heat, stir together water and sugar until sugar dissolves. Add cranberries, cook until berries are soft. Remove from heat before they pop. Pour the mixture into a colander; cool completely.

To assemble, wrap about one teaspoonful of set chocolate mixture around 1 whole cranberry to cover. Place on a tray lined with waxed paper. Repeat until all cranberries are wrapped in chocolate. Refrigerate truffles for at least 20 minutes.

Roll chilled truffles in ground toasted hazelnuts. Place truffles in candy papers. Refrigerate in an airtight container until ready to serve. (Truffles will keep about one week.)

New Year's Resolution Party

Black Currant Linzer Wreaths
Chocolate Truffle Cake with Espresso Crème Anglaise
Pumpkin Crème Brulée with Caramel Cages
Brandied Camembert
White Zinfandel Poached Pears with
Blueberry Cassis Coulis
Champagne

New Year's is traditionally a time for resolutions and fresh starts, and with it the opportunity to set new goals and dream about new possibilities. This party inaugurates a festive year proposing five recipes guaranteed to bring guests back year after year.

Ring in the year with elegance! Bring the opulence of gold to your table by wrapping the Chocolate Truffle Cake with a wide gold ribbon and topping individual Pumpkin Crème Brulées with finely woven golden cages. Then display all these desserts on a shimmering tablecloth.

Black Currant Linzer Wreaths

In the tradition of the classic linzertorte, this hazelnut version is a sweet and pretty addition to any buffet table year round. *Makes about 2 dozen.*

Pastry
  1½ cups all-purpose flour, sifted
  ¼ cup granulated sugar
  ¼ cup firmly packed light brown sugar
  ½ teaspoon baking powder
  2 tablespoons finely grated lemon peel
  ½ teaspoon ground cinnamon
  ¼ teaspoon ground cloves
  Pinch of salt
  ⅔ cup unsalted butter, chilled and cut into pieces
  4 egg yolks
  2 teaspoons ice water
  ¾ cup ground hazelnuts

Filling
  1 cup black currant preserves

Glaze
  1 egg
  1 teaspoon milk
  Confectioners' sugar

For pastry, combine flour, granulated sugar, brown sugar, baking powder, lemon peel, cinnamon, cloves, and salt in a large bowl. Cut in butter using a pastry cutter or two knives used scissor-fashion until mixture resembles coarse crumbs. Stir together egg yolks and water in a small bowl. Stir in hazelnuts. Add hazelnut mixture to flour mixture; mix until pastry forms a ball. Wrap dough in plastic and refrigerate for 1 hour.

Preheat oven to 375°. Divide dough into 2 pieces, one piece using three fourths of the dough. Roll larger piece out on a lightly floured surface to ¼-inch thickness. Cut dough using a 2-inch round, scalloped-edge cookie cutter. Transfer cookies to baking sheets. With remaining dough, form a small amount of dough (about dime size) into a ball. Roll dough between lightly floured hands into a 5-inch long rope. Form rope into a circle and place on top of a cookie round. Fill cookie center with 1 heaping teaspoon preserves. Repeat procedure with remaining cookie dough and preserves.

For glaze, beat together egg and milk in a small cup. Brush glaze over pastry. Bake for 10 to 12 minutes, or until pastry is golden brown and filling is bubbly. Cool cookies on baking sheet for 5 minutes. Transfer cookies to a wire rack; cool completely before serving. Dust cookies with confectioners' sugar.

Pumpkin Crème Brulée with Caramel Cages and Chocolate Truffle Cake with Espresso Crème Anglaise

Chocolate Truffle Cake with Espresso Crème Anglaise

This decadent chocolate cake is ideal for special occasions. *Serves 8 to 10.*

16 ounces semi-sweet chocolate
½ cup unsalted butter
1½ teaspoons granulated sugar
1½ teaspoons all-purpose flour
1 teaspoon hot water
4 egg yolks, at room temperature
4 egg whites, at room temperature

Espresso Crème Anglaise
1 Espresso Crème Anglaise recipe, see page 140.

Garnish
3 ounces semi-sweet chocolate
Confectioners' sugar

Preheat oven to 425°. Grease bottom of an 8-inch springform pan. Melt 16 ounces chocolate and butter in top of a double boiler set over simmering water, stirring until smooth. Remove from heat. Add 1½ teaspoons sugar, flour, and hot water to chocolate; blend well. Add 4 egg yolks, one at a time, blending well after each addition.

Beat egg whites in a clean bowl with clean beaters until stiff. Fold egg whites into chocolate mixture, one third at a time. Gently pour mixture into prepared pan. Bake for 15 minutes. Cake will appear very undercooked in center. Cool completely (as cake cools, it will sink a bit in the middle). Chill until ready to serve.

Prepare Espresso Crème Anglaise as directed.

For garnish, melt 3 ounces semi-sweet chocolate in top of a double boiler set over simmering water, stirring until smooth. Spread melted chocolate into a 1¼-inch layer over a chilled marble slab or iced countertop. Let chocolate set for 2 hours at room temperature or until set and has lost its gloss. To make shavings or curls, pull a sharp straight-edged knife held at an angle across chocolate layer. (The more horizontally the knife is held, the larger the curls will be.) Lift shavings with a spatula (do not use hands or chocolate will melt) and transfer shavings to top of cake. Pile shavings on top of cake. Lightly sift confectioners' sugar over shavings. Serve cake with prepared Espresso Crème Anglaise.

Pumpkin Crème Brulée with Caramel Cages

Although the name is French, crème brulée is actually British in origin. To make a traditional "burnt cream," simply sprinkle 2 tablespoons dark brown sugar over each serving. Then broil until the sugar caramelizes.
Serves 10.

3 cups whipping cream
2 teaspoons vanilla
6 egg yolks, at room temperature
¼ cup plus 2 tablespoons granulated sugar
¾ cup finely puréed cooked pumpkin
1 tablespoon maple syrup
1 tablespoon cognac
¼ teaspoon ground ginger
¼ teaspoon ground cinnamon
¼ teaspoon ground nutmeg
Pinch of salt

Caramel Cage
1 cup granulated sugar
¼ cup plus 1 tablespoon cold water
⅛ teaspoon cream of tartar
Vegetable oil

Preheat oven to 350°. For crème brulée, scald whipping cream in a medium, heavy saucepan over medium-high heat. Remove from heat; stir in vanilla. Beat egg yolks and ¼ cup plus 2 tablespoons granulated sugar in a large bowl until thick. Beat pumpkin, maple syrup, cognac, ginger, cinnamon, nutmeg, and salt, into egg mixture; blend well. Slowly whisk in hot cream. Pour mixture into ten ½-cup ramekins. Skim any foam off the top of the custards. Place ramekins in a baking dish and pour boiling water into baking dish until water comes halfway up sides of ramekins. Bake for 45 to 60 minutes or until set. Cool completely. Chill for at least 8 hours or overnight.

For Caramel Cage, combine 1 cup granulated sugar and ¼ cup water in a heavy saucepan over medium-high heat. Bring mixture to a boil. Do not stir. Boil for 3 minutes. Dissolve cream of tartar in remaining 1 tablespoon water in a cup; add to sugar mixture. Continue cooking without stirring until mixture is a light caramel color, about 8 minutes.

Select metal bowls that will completely fit over the crème brulée dishes. Oil the bowls well with vegetable oil. Using a teaspoon, weave the caramel mixture in long threads from one side of the bowl to the other, making a free-form design. When the desired design is achieved, cool the caramel completely. Carefully release the caramel form from the edges of the bowls and remove. The hardened caramel will resemble cages. Place over crème brulée.

Note: Do not attempt to make caramel cages on hot, humid days.

Brandied Camembert

Serves 6 to 8.

8 ounces Camembert cheese, rind removed and cut into pieces
½ cup unsalted butter, softened and cut into pieces
2 tablespoons brandy
½ cup sliced almonds, toasted
Unsalted crackers or fresh fruit

Combine cheese, butter, and brandy in a food processor until smooth. Form mixture into a ball or log shape. Place nuts in a shallow dish. Roll cheese in toasted nuts, pressing them into the surface of the cheese. Wrap tightly in plastic wrap and refrigerate. Remove from refrigerator 20 minutes before serving. Serve with crackers or fruit.

Note: Brandied Camembert keeps well for 2 weeks in the refrigerator.

White Zinfandel Poached Pears with Blueberry-Cassis Coulis

A striking color contrast of pale pink and deep blue makes this a distinctive dessert. Serve chilled poached pears on a bed of baby lettuce for a light summer salad.
Serves 8.

6 cups white zinfandel wine
3 cups granulated sugar
¼ cup plus 2 tablespoons fresh lemon juice
2 teaspoons finely grated lemon peel
8 large firm Bosc pears, peeled with stems intact

Blueberry-Cassis Coulis
½ cup water
½ cup crème de cassis
3 tablespoons fresh lemon juice
2 tablespoons cornstarch
2 cups fresh or frozen and thawed blueberries
2 tablespoons granulated sugar
Mint leaves

Heat wine, 3 cups sugar, ¼ cup plus 2 tablespoons lemon juice, and lemon peel in a heavy, 3-quart saucepan over low heat, stirring occasionally until sugar dissolves. Increase heat to medium-high and simmer. Cut bottom of each pear to flatten. Add pears to wine mixture. Reduce heat and simmer until just tender when pierced with a knife, about 30 to 50 minutes. Transfer pears to a large bowl using a slotted spoon. Cool pears and poaching liquid separately. Pour cool poaching liquid over pears. Cover and refrigerate overnight.

For coulis, combine water, crème de cassis, 3 tablespoons lemon juice, and cornstarch in a heavy 3-quart saucepan over low heat. Stir until cornstarch dissolves. Add blueberries. Increase heat to medium and stir until sauce thickens and coats the back of a spoon, about 5 minutes. Transfer sauce to a blender; puree until smooth. Strain sauce through a fine sieve. Add remaining 2 tablespoons granulated sugar to taste, one tablespoon at a time.

To serve, drain pears. Pour Blueberry-Cassis Coulis onto individual serving plates or serving platter. Stand pears in sauce. Garnish with mint leaves.

Super Bowl Sunday Brunch

French Custard Toast with Fresh Berries
Glazed Bacon Spirals
Winter Compote
Orange-Cranberry Spritzer

At the end of every January is the *unofficial* holiday known as Super Bowl Sunday. Huddled in front of the television are football's biggest fans and on the sidelines are the supporters who after a season of being alone on Sundays figure if you can't beat em'—join em'!

Before kickoff serve a terrific winter brunch with several twists on old favorites. The table—not the television—becomes the focus of attention during pregame activities. The reward for waiting for the showdown between the A.F.C. and the N.F.C. is a scrumptious menu consisting of French Custard Toast with Fresh Berries, Glazed Bacon Spirals, Winter Compote, and Orange-Cranberry Spritzers. This collection of recipes would also make an excellent Christmas morning or New Year's Day brunch.

French Custard Toast with Fresh Berries

French Toast, or *Pain Perdu* (literally "lost bread"), is a delicious way to transform day old bread into a heavenly morning treat.
Serves 6.

12 1½-inch slices cinnamon-raisin bread
4 eggs
2 egg yolks
4 cups half and half
⅔ cup granulated sugar
1 tablespoon vanilla
1½ teaspoons finely grated lemon peel
1½ teaspoons finely grated orange peel
1 teaspoon freshly grated nutmeg
12 tablespoons unsalted butter
Confectioners' sugar
1 cup fresh blueberries, rinsed
1 cup fresh raspberries, rinsed
1 cup fresh strawberries, rinsed
Maple syrup (optional)

Arrange bread slices in two 9 × 13-inch baking pans; set aside.

Whisk eggs, egg yolks, half and half, granulated sugar, vanilla, lemon peel, orange peel, and nutmeg in a large bowl until blended. Pour over bread. Let soak for 5 minutes; turn slices over. Cover pans with plastic wrap. Refrigerate for 3 hours or overnight.

Melt 4 tablespoons of the butter in a heavy skillet over medium-high heat. Add bread and fry until golden brown, about 5 minutes per side. Do not undercook or middle will not be completely set. Transfer to heated serving dishes. Repeat procedure using remaining butter and bread. Sift confectioners' sugar over slices. Serve with blueberries, raspberries, strawberries, and maple syrup, if desired.

Glazed Bacon Spirals

Serves 6.

1 pound thick-sliced bacon
½ cup firmly packed light brown sugar
¼ cup dry sherry
2 tablespoons Dijon mustard

Preheat oven to 375°. Twist the bacon slices into spirals; arrange them in rows on rack of a broiler pan. Secure spirals with metal skewers laying across top and bottom ends of bacon. Bake for 15 to 20 minutes or until crisp.

Meanwhile, combine brown sugar, sherry, and mustard in a small bowl. Brush glaze over bacon spirals. Bake for 5 minutes more. Brush additional glaze over spirals. Bake for 5 minutes, more. Serve warm.

French Custard Toast with Glazed Bacon Spirals, Fresh Berries, and Orange-Cranberry Spritzers

Winter Compote

A light and refreshing winter fruit salad.
Serves 6.

⅔ cup granulated sugar
⅔ cup water
¾ cup coarsely chopped dried apricots
½ cup fresh cranberries
2 naval oranges, peeled and cut into segments
1 large pink grapefruit, peeled and cut into segments

Combine sugar and water in a small saucepan over medium-high heat. Bring mixture to a boil, stirring constantly until sugar dissolves. Add apricots and cranberries. Simmer until cranberries just begin to pop, about 5 minutes. Transfer mixture to a small bowl. Cover and chill completely.

Combine orange and grapefruit segments in a medium bowl. Stir cranberry mixture into orange-grapefruit mixture. Chill until ready to serve.

Orange-Cranberry Spritzer

For a nonalcoholic drink, you can omit the vodka.
Serves 6.

2¼ cups fresh orange juice
2¼ cups cranberry juice cocktail
1½ cups fresh grapefruit juice
1 cup vodka (optional)
2 cups seltzer water or club soda, chilled
Shaved ice

In a large pitcher combine orange juice, cranberry juice, grapefruit juice, and vodka, if desired. Stir in seltzer water or club soda. Pour into large glasses filled with shaved ice.

Fireside Desserts for Two

Coeur À La Crème with Red Berry Purée
Oranges in Riesling
Champagne

Valentine's day casts a romantic spell over February. This menu provides everything you need for an intimate and elegant celebration for two: Coeur À La Crème with Red Berry Purée and Oranges in Riesling. Set the table with your best china, crystal, and silver. Don't forget the soft music, flowers, and candlelight to complete the recipe for romance.

Coeur À La Crème with Red Berry Purée

Food stylist Alice Hart created this recipe for her Los Angeles cooking class. This classic dessert is made in a special coeur à la crème mold which has holes in the bottom of it to drain the excess whey.
Serves 4 to 6.

1 quart ice water
1 tablespoon fresh lemon juice
Pinch of baking soda
1 8-ounce package cream cheese, softened
½ cup small curd cottage cheese
¾ cup confectioners' sugar
2 teaspoons vanilla
Peel of one lemon, finely grated
1½ cups whipping cream
Sauce
1 10-ounce package frozen sweetened strawberries, thawed
1 10-ounce package frozen sweetened raspberries, thawed
1 tablespoon cornstarch
1 teaspoon fresh lemon juice
¼ cup kirsch (optional)
1 pint fresh strawberries or raspberries, rinsed

Combine water, lemon juice, and baking soda in a bowl. Cut a piece of cheesecloth large enough to line a 3-cup coeur à la crème mold and extend at least 2 inches beyond edges of mold. Soak cloth in water until ready to use.

Beat cream cheese and cottage cheese in a medium mixing bowl on medium speed until smooth. Beat in sugar, vanilla, and lemon peel. Beat whipping cream in a chilled bowl with chilled beaters until stiff. Fold whipped cream into cream cheese mixture.

Line mold with wrung-out cheesecloth. Gently spoon cheese mixture into mold. Smooth top with back of a spoon. Fold cheesecloth over top to cover. Place mold on a wire rack set over a plate to drain. Refrigerate at least 8 hours or overnight.

For sauce, drain off excess liquid from thawed berries into a 2-cup measuring cup; reserve fruit. Add enough water to berry liquid to yield 1¾ cups fluid. Stir in cornstarch. Transfer fruit juice to a small saucepan over medium heat. Bring mixture to a boil; reduce heat and simmer for 5 minutes. Cool. Purée reserved strawberries and raspberries in a blender. Blend in cooled fruit juice, lemon juice, and kirsch, if desired. Press sauce through a fine sieve set over a small bowl.

To assemble, unfold cheese cloth. Unmold coeur à la crème onto a serving platter. Carefully remove cheesecloth. Garnish with fresh berries. Serve sauce separately.

Note: For individual servings, line six ½-cup coeur à la crème molds with cheesecloth.

Oranges in Riesling

This light dessert doubles easily for a perfect ending to a Chinese or Asian dinner.
Serves 2.

2 large navel oranges
⅓ cup Riesling wine
⅓ cup water
3½ tablespoons granulated sugar

Pare a piece of orange peel 3 inches long and ½-inch wide from one of the oranges. Cut peel into thin julienned strips; set aside. Remove remaining peel and membranes from oranges. Separate orange sections.

Combine wine, water, and sugar in a small, heavy saucepan over low heat, stirring constantly until sugar dissolves; bring to a simmer. Add orange sections. Remove from heat. Stir in julienned orange peel. Cool to room temperature. Place oranges in individual serving bowls. Spoon riesling syrup over oranges. Cover and refrigerate for 3 hours or overnight. Serve chilled.

Coeur À La Crème with Red Berry Purée and Champagne

Fondue Fantasy

Chocolate Fondue
Orange-Caramel Fondue
Crystalized Ginger Pound Cake
Tangerine Pound Cake
Hazelnut Biscotti
Hot Buttered Rum

Bring out your old fondue pot, the fondue party has returned. Warm up a chilly night after an exhilarating day of skiing with two special dessert fondues and a rich mug of creamy Hot Buttered Rum. This menu is easy to prepare whether made at home or at a ski resort condo. Any variety of dippers will work: Crystalized Ginger and Tangerine Pound Cake cubes, Hazelnut Biscotti, glacéed apricots, fresh fruit, and pretzels provide a variety of color, flavors, and textures to a fondue menu, and—best of all—can all be prepared ahead.

Set the scene around a roaring fire. Table settings are minimum, just napkins, serving plates for dippers, fondue forks, and mugs.

Chocolate Fondue, Glacéed Fruits, and Hazelnut Biscotti

Chocolate Fondue

What could be better on a cold winter's night than a smooth, warm chocolate dip?
Makes about 2 cups.

> 6 ounces bittersweet chocolate, chopped
> 6 ounces milk chocolate, chopped
> ½ cup whipping cream
> 3 tablespoons desired liqueur such as créme de cacao, Grand Marnier, amaretto, or light rum
> Assorted dippers such as glacéed fruits, pretzels, fresh fruit, and whole large nuts

Combine bittersweet chocolate, milk chocolate, and whipping cream in a heavy saucepan over low heat, stirring until smooth. (This may be made to this point and reheated). Just before serving stir in desired liqueur. The mixture should be thick, but if it is too thick add more whipping cream, one tablespoon at a time, until sauce achieves desired consistency. Transfer chocolate mixture to fondue pot. Serve with assorted dippers.

Orange-Caramel Fondue

The recipe for this creamy citrus sauce easily doubles. It will keep for several days stored in a glass jar in the refrigerator. To reheat, set jar in a saucepan filled with water over low heat.
Makes about 2½ cups.

> 2 cups granulated sugar
> 1 cup firmly packed brown sugar
> ⅔ unsalted butter, softened, cut into pieces
> 1 cup whipping cream
> 2 teaspoons vanilla
> 2 tablespoons finely grated orange peel

Combine sugar, brown sugar, butter, and whipping cream in a heavy, 2-quart saucepan over medium-low heat, stirring constantly until sugar dissolves. Increase heat to medium-high and bring mixture to a boil. Cook until a candy thermometer reaches 225°. Remove from heat. Stir in vanilla and orange peel. Transfer to fondue pot. Serve with assorted dippers.

Crystalized Ginger Pound Cake

Makes 1 loaf.

1 cup all-purpose flour
1½ teaspoons baking powder
1 cup plus 2 tablespoons granulated sugar
¾ cup unsalted butter, softened
3 eggs, at room temperature
¼ cup plus 2 tablespoons sour cream
1 teaspoon vanilla
4 ounces (about ½ cup) crystalized ginger, coarsely
    chopped
½ cup all-purpose flour

Butter and lightly flour a 9 × 5½-inch loaf pan; set aside. Preheat oven to 350°. Combine 1 cup flour and baking powder in a small bowl; set aside. Beat sugar and butter in a large mixing bowl on medium speed until light and fluffy. Reduce speed to low and beat in eggs, one at a time, blending well after each addition. Combine sour cream and vanilla in a cup. Add flour mixture and sour cream alternately into batter and beat till well combined, beginning and ending with flour mixture. Increase speed to high and beat until smooth. Toss together ginger and ½ cup flour in a small bowl. Fold ginger and flour mixture into batter. Pour batter into prepared pan. Bake for 50 to 60 minutes or until cake tester inserted in center comes out clean. Cool in pan for 10 minutes. Remove cake from pan and cool completely on a wire rack. Wrap cake in plastic wrap and refrigerate overnight. To serve, cut into slices or 1-inch cubes for fondue.

Note: Crystalized Ginger Pound Cake can be refrigerated up to 1 week or frozen for 1 month.

Tangerine Pound Cake

Take advantage of winter's citrus in this tangy pound cake. To serve it as a fondue dipper, cut the cake into 1-inch cubes. Tangerine Pound Cake wrapped in plastic will keep several days in the refrigerator.
Makes 1 loaf.

Peel of 1½ tangerines, finely chopped
1 cup granulated sugar
1½ cups unsalted butter, softened
2 eggs, at room temperature
1¼ cups all-purpose flour
¼ teaspoon baking powder
1 teaspoon baking soda
¼ teaspoon salt
¼ cup plus 2 tablespoons buttermilk

Grease and lightly flour a 7 × ½-inch loaf pan; set aside. Preheat oven to 350°. Combine tangerine peel and sugar in a small bowl; set aside. Beat butter in a medium mixing bowl on medium speed until smooth. Gradually add sugar mixture; beat until light and fluffy. Add eggs, one at a time, blending well after each addition. Combine flour, baking powder, baking soda, and salt in a bowl. Add flour and buttermilk alternately into sugar mixture and beat till well combined, beginning and ending with flour mixture. Pour batter into prepared pan. Bake for 50 to 60 minutes, or until cake tester inserted in center comes out clean. Cool in pan for 10 minutes. Remove cake from pan and cool completely on a wire rack. Serve at room temperature.

Hazelnut Biscotti

Enjoy these "twice baked" cookies with a steaming cup of cappuccino or a sweet dessert wine such as Marsala. *Makes 6 dozen.*

2 cups granulated sugar
2 cups coarsely chopped hazelnuts
1 cup unsalted butter, melted
¼ cup aniseed
¼ cup anisette
2 tablespoons water
2 teaspoons vanilla
6 eggs, at room temperature
5½ cups all-purpose flour
1 tablespoon baking powder

Mix sugar, nuts, melted butter, aniseed, anisette, water, and vanilla in a large bowl. Add eggs, one at a time, stirring well after each addition. Combine flour and baking powder in a medium bowl; stir into nut mixture, 1 cup at a time. Cover bowl with plastic wrap and refrigerate for 3 hours.

Grease baking sheets. Preheat oven to 375°. Divide dough into five equal pieces. Shape each piece into a long roll, ½-inch high and 2 inches wide. Place each roll on prepared baking sheets, four inches apart. Bake for 20 minutes or until firm to touch. Cool on baking sheets for 30 minutes. Maintain oven temperature at 375°. Cut each roll into ½- to ¾-inch thick slices. Arrange slices cut side down on baking sheets. Bake for 5 to 7 minutes more or until light brown on each side. Cool completely on wire racks. Store biscotti at room temperature in an airtight container.

Variation: For Chocolate-Dipped Biscotti, melt 6 ounces semi-sweet chocolate in top of a double boiler set over simmering water, stirring until smooth. Remove from heat. Dip the long bottom edge of each cookie into melted chocolate. Place Chocolate Dipped Biscotti on a baking sheet lined with waxed paper. Refrigerate until chocolate is set, about 15 minutes. Serve immediately or wrap cookies tightly in plastic wrap and store in a cool, dry place for up to 2 days.

Hot Buttered Rum

Beware! Much of the ice cream base for this drink may be eaten directly from the freezer before it ever makes into mugs for serving. Fortunately this recipe doubles easily. *Serves 12 to 18.*

1 cup unsalted butter, softened
½ cup firmly packed dark brown sugar
½ cup confectioners' sugar, sifted
1 teaspoon ground nutmeg
1 teaspoon ground cinnamon
1 pint high-quality vanilla ice cream, softened
Dark rum
Boiling water
Cinnamon sticks

Beat butter, brown sugar, confectioners' sugar, nutmeg, and cinnamon in a large mixing bowl until smooth. Beat in ice cream. Turn ice cream mixture into a 4-cup freezer container. Seal and freeze until ice cream is set (mixture will not be solid), about 4 hours. To serve, spoon 3 to 4 tablespoons ice cream mixture into a mug. Add 3 tablespoons rum and ½ cup boiling water to each mug. Stir well. Garnish with a cinnamon stick.

8

Master Recipes

Crème Fraîche

Makes about 2 cups.

½ cup sour cream
2 cups whipping cream, preferably not ultrapasterized

Place sour cream in a bowl. Thin sour cream with a little whipping cream; then add remaining whipping cream. Pour mixture into a clean glass jar, cover loosely, and let thicken at room temperature. This will take about 4 to 12 hours, depending upon warmth of room. Cover thickened mixture tightly and refrigerate. Chill completely.

Variation: For Lime Crème Fraîche, add 1½ teaspoons finely grated lime peel and 1 tablespoon fresh lime juice to each 1 cup of Crème Fraîche.

Crème Anglaise

Makes about 2¼ cups.

6 egg yolks, at room temperature
⅓ cup plus 2 tablespoons granulated sugar
Pinch of salt
1 cup whipping cream
¾ cup milk
1 tablespoon vanilla

Whisk together egg yolks, sugar, and salt in a medium mixing bowl until thickened. Combine whipping cream and milk in heavy, 1½-quart saucepan over medium-low heat; scald until bubbles form around the edge of the pan. Gradually whisk about 1 cup of hot milk mixture into egg yolk mixture. Return egg and milk mixture to saucepan. Continue cooking over medium-low heat, stirring constantly until sauce thickens and coats the back of a metal spoon (do not boil), about 2 to 4 minutes. Remove from heat. Stir in vanilla. Strain custard into a bowl. Press plastic wrap directly onto surface of Crème Anglaise to prevent a skin from forming. Cool completely. Refrigerate until ready to use.

Note: Crème Anglaise can be served hot, warm, or cool.

Variations:

Maple Crème Anglaise: For Maple Crème Anglaise, delete granulated sugar and milk. Whisk ¾ cup maple syrup together with egg yolks. Heat whipping cream as directed and add to maple syrup mixture. Continue as directed.

Espresso Crème Anglaise: For Espresso Crème Anglaise, stir 3 tablespoons instant espresso powder into hot Crème Anglaise until espresso dissolves.

Pistachio Crème Anglaise: For Pistachio Crème Anglaise, fold ½ cup finely chopped, toasted pistachios into warm Crème Anglaise.

Sweetened Whipped Cream

Makes about 2¼ cups.

1 cup whipping cream
2 tablespoons confectioners' sugar
1 teaspoon vanilla

Beat whipping cream, confectioners' sugar, and vanilla in a chilled bowl with chilled beaters until stiff. Cover and refrigerate until ready to use.

Puff Pastry

Makes about 1 pound.

2 cups all-purpose flour
½ teaspoon salt
1 cup unsalted butter, chilled and cut into pieces
⅓ to ½ cup ice water

Combine flour and salt in a large bowl. Cut in butter, using a pastry blender or two knives used scissor-fashion until butter is pea-sized and flour resembles coarse crumbs. Stir in ⅓ cup ice water. Add additional water, 1 tablespoon at a time, until mixture forms a soft dough. Form dough into a ball. Dust dough lightly with flour. Wrap dough in waxed paper and refrigerate for 1 hour.

Roll dough out on a lightly floured surface into a 12 × 6-inch rectangle. Mentally divide rectangle into lower, middle, and upper thirds (three 4 × 6-inch sections); lightly mark off sections with fingertip. Fold upper third of rectangle over the center third and the lower third over the top. (The dough should be folded like a business letter; there should be three distinct layers now.) Use fingers to square corners and even all edges. With open side facing you, roll dough out again to a 12 × 6-inch rectangle. Again, fold into thirds. This completes 2 turns. Repeat rolling and folding procedure two more times, always starting with the open end facing you. Wrap folded dough in waxed paper and refrigerate for at least 30 minutes or up to 3 days. Use puff pastry direct from refrigerator as directed in recipe.

Ladyfingers

Makes about 3 dozen.

3 egg yolks, at room temperature
3 tablespoons granulated sugar
1½ teaspoons vanilla
½ cup cake flour, sifted
Pinch of salt
3 egg whites, at room temperature
¼ teaspoon cream of tartar
3 tablespoons granulated sugar
½ to 1 cup confectioners' sugar

Grease and lightly flour two baking sheets; set aside. Preheat oven to 325°. Beat egg yolks and 3 tablespoons granulated sugar in a medium mixing bowl on medium-high speed until mixture forms a ribbon when beaters are lifted, about 5 minutes. Add vanilla; set aside.

Beat egg whites and cream of tartar in medium mixing bowl on high speed until frothy. Gradually add 3 tablespoons granulated sugar, beating until stiff. Fold egg white mixture, one third at a time, into egg yolk mixture, blending well after each addition. Spoon batter into a pastry bag fitted with a plain ½-inch round tip. Pipe batter on prepared baking sheets, holding pastry bag at a 45-degree angle, into 3½- to 5-inch long Ladyfingers. Pipe rows of Ladyfingers until baking sheets are full. Leave at least ½ to ¾ inches between each ladyfinger. Dust with confectioners' sugar using a sieve. Bake for 10 to 12 minutes, or until just barely colored, but springs back when lightly touched. Cool on baking sheets for 1 minute. Transfer Ladyfingers to a wire rack. Cool completely. Use Ladyfingers as directed in specific recipe.

Note: Store ladyfingers at room temperature in an airtight container between layers of waxed paper for no longer than 2 days. Ladyfingers can be frozen for up to 10 days.

Pâte Sable

One 9- or 10-inch tart shell.

1 cup all-purpose flour
½ cup plus 2 tablespoons granulated sugar
Pinch of salt
½ cup unsalted butter, chilled and cut into pieces
1 egg yolk, chilled
1 tablespoon ice water

Combine flour, sugar, and salt in a medium bowl. Cut in butter using a pastry blender or two knives used scissor-fashion. Stir in egg yolk and water until just moistened. Form dough into a ball. Pat dough into bottom and up sides of a 9- or 10-inch tart pan with removable bottom. Cover and refrigerate for at least 1 hour.

Preheat oven to 350°. Prick pastry shell with a fork at ½-inch intervals over the bottom and sides. Bake for 20 to 25 minutes or until pale golden. Cool completely.

Basic Dessert Crêpes

Crêpes are delicate, thin pancakes which can be made in advance. Fill this sweet version with mousse, pastry cream, ice cream, flavored whipped cream, or fruit compote. If you prefer a lighter crêpe, use half milk and half water.
Makes about 20 crêpes.

½ cup plus 2 tablespoons water
½ cup milk
3 eggs
2 tablespoons unsalted butter, melted and cooled
1 cup all-purpose flour
2½ tablespoons granulated sugar
Pinch of salt
Vegetable oil

Combine water, milk, eggs, and melted butter in a blender or food processor; process at low speed until just blended. Stir together flour, sugar, and salt in a small bowl. Add flour mixture, one third at a time, to milk mixture, blending at low speed after each addition. Scrape sides of container after each addition. Blend at high speed for 1 minute. Scrape sides of container again to dislodge any remaining flour. Blend for 2 to 5 seconds more. Cover the batter and refrigerate for at least one hour. (The batter may be made up to 24 hours in advance.

To cook crêpes, lightly grease an 8-inch crêpe pan or non-stick skillet with vegetable oil. Heat the pan over medium-high heat until a drop of water sizzles in pan. Gently stir the batter. Pour in enough batter to just coat the pan, about 2 to 3 tablespoons, tilting and swirling until bottom is just covered with thin layer of batter. Pour off any excess batter back into container. Cook until underside of crêpe is golden brown, about 45 to 60 seconds. Turn crêpe to cook other side, about 10 to 15 seconds more, not to brown the second side but to ensure the crêpe is well cooked. (This un-browned side will be the inside of a rolled or filled crêpe.)

Cool crêpe on a wire rack. Place a square piece of waxed paper between each crêpe. Repeat with remaining batter, stirring occasionally. Adjust heat and add more oil as necessary.

Variation:

Hazelnut Crêpes: For Hazelnut Crêpes, prepare basic dessert crepe batter as directed, but add 3 tablespoons toasted, skinned, and ground hazelnuts to flour mixture.

Note: Store crêpes tightly wrapped in foil or plastic for up to two days in the refrigerator. To freeze crêpes, tightly wrap 4 to 6 crêpes in aluminum foil. Seal each set of aluminum foil-wrapped crêpes in a freezer bag. The edges of frozen crêpes are brittle, so handle them with care. To thaw, remove them from freezer bag and thaw in refrigerator. Crêpes will keep up to four months in the freezer. To reheat, place crêpes, one at a time, in crêpe pan over low heat for about 5 seconds per side.

Additional Styling Credits

PRETTY SPRING PARTIES
Mid-Morning Muffin Break
    Tableware by Tesoro
Caribbean Anniversary Romantique
    Tableware and Tablecloth by Tesoro
A Charity Auction Dessert Buffet
    Tableware by Steve's
Elegant Easter Brunch
    Tableware by Tesoro
    Flower Vase by Steve's
Fiesta Cinco de Mayo
    Tableware by Tesoro
A Bridesmaids' Tea
    Silver Tea Set, Platters, Tableware, and Tablecloth by Tesoro

BREEZY SUMMER PARTIES
A Father's Day Brunch
    Tableware and Tablecloth by Tesoro
A Mad Hatter's Tea
    Silverware by Blueprint
    Tableware and Tablecloth by Tesoro
Cool Down Dessert Party
    Glassware by Tesoro
Poolside Refresher
    Tableware, Glassware, Tablecloth, and Candle Holder by Tesoro
A Sensational Baby Shower
    Platter, Server, and Tablecloth by Tesoro
    Silver Baby Items, Teddy Bear, and Wooden Animals by Mise En Place
A Summer Soirée
    Tableware and Tablecloth by Tesoro

ELEGANT AUTUMN PARTIES
European Dessert Soirée
    Marble Table and Glass Platter by Art Options
    Cups and Platters by Tesoro
Back to School Brunch
    Table and Tableware by Art Options
Oktoberfest
    Tableware and Tablecloth by Tesoro
Tricks or Treats
    Platter, Tablecloth, and Server by Tesoro
    Halloween Creatures by Mise En Place

New Orleans Fête
    Tableware by Tesoro
After Theatre Rendezvous
    Tableware by Tesoro

FESTIVE WINTER PARTIES
A Nutcracker Tea
    Tableware by Tesoro
A Tree Trimming Get-Together
    Tableware and Candlestick Holders by Tosoro
New Year's Resolution Party
    Tableware by Tesoro
Super Bowl Sunday Brunch
    Tableware by Tesoro
Fireside Desserts for Two
    Tableware and Placemats by Art Options
Fondue Fantasy
    Brandy Snifters by Geary's

PROP SOURCES
Art Options
2507 Main Street
Santa Monica, CA 90405
(213) 392-9099

Blueprint
8366 Beverly Boulevard
Los Angeles, CA 90048
(213) 653-2439

Geary's
437 North Beverly Boulevard
Beverly Hills, CA 90210
(213) 273-4741

Mise En Place
2120 North Hillhurst Avenue
Los Angeles, CA 90027
(213) 662-1334

Steve's
9530 Little Santa Monica Boulevard
Beverly Hills, CA 90210
(213) 274-6567

Tesoro
319 South Robertson Boulevard
Los Angeles, CA 90048
(213) 273-9090

Index